2   1.⁰⁰

HOT
ITALIAN
DISH

HOT ITALIAN DISH

VICTORIA GOTTI

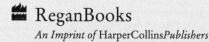

ReganBooks

An Imprint of HarperCollins*Publishers*

HarperCollins books may be purchased for educational, business, or sales promotional use. For information please write: Special Markets Department, HarperCollins Publishers Inc., 10 East 53rd Street, New York, NY 10022.

FIRST EDITION

Designed by Anthony Colletti

Printed on acid-free paper

Library of Congress Cataloging-in-Publication Data has been applied for.

ISBN 13: 978-0-06-085168-2
ISBN 10: 0-06-085168-6

06 07 08 09 10 WBG/QWF 10 9 8 7 6 5 4 3 2 1

To my mom, Victoria.
Thank you for years of invaluable knowledge
of all things culinary.

CONTENTS

PREFACE

Kitchen Princess ∽

I had always wanted to learn how to cook. Credit watching my mother in the kitchen for my obsessive love of food, but ever since I was seven or eight, I have been fascinated with preparing meals and watching the finished product being devoured by an army of hungry family members and friends.

I usually put so much effort and time into my meal because it's my way of communicating with those I hold near and dear. For instance, even though I'm a single working mom (with three careers, mind you!) I still make time to cook a homemade meal for the three most important men in my life—my sons. It's the least I can do to show how much I appreciate them and let them know I love them dearly. Not only do I put a hearty and delicious meal on the table every night, I also let the boys take turns choosing their favorite dishes. Carmine, my oldest, loves cheese ravioli and pomodoro sauce, while my middle son John enjoys an extensive array of homemade soups like chicken noodle and beef barley. As for Frank, my youngest, before he went on a diet he was a meat and potatoes kind of guy. He enjoyed my beef stew so much, he usually had three or four helpings!

Watching my loved ones, especially my children, practically lick their plates clean after a meal I've prepared is gratitude enough for me. Hearing them brag to friends, classmates, and other family members about a certain dish I prepared last night or last week is the best form of praise I could ever hope for. The appreciation and respect I garner from cooking forces me to spend more time in the kitchen than I ever imagined. Sometimes, if I find myself restless late at night, I'll grab my terry robe, tiptoe down the stairs, and bake a few dozen cupcakes and a fresh loaf of banana bread. It's pretty random, but these after-hours cooking sessions allow the kids to enjoy an incredible snack on their way to school and a sweet treat at lunch later on that day.

Sadly, most women view cooking as a chore, only because there doesn't seem to be enough hours in the day for them to do all the necessary tasks to keep their households running like an army barracks. The key factor that most women just don't get is that cooking a few favorite dishes for their family is not in any way a chore if it's done with love, tenderness, and care. Cooking is also sexy—even the most testosterone-driven man can grow weak in the knees for a plate of delicious pasta pomodoro or beef Wellington.

I wrote this cookbook as a testimonial to all that I have learned over the years while navigating my way around the kitchen, and hearing, learning, tasting, and, yes, observing from the sidelines. I enjoy watching each and every "customer" sample, then dig into my sometimes hard-to-make homemade recipes. They let me know how satisfied they are by sending me back an empty plate.

Cooking is like painting. The kitchen counter, stove, and oven are my canvas and serve as my workspace, and the colorful vegetables and ingredients are my paints. Kitchen utensils such as wooden spoons, colanders, and pots, serve as my paintbrushes. I scour my recipe books constantly looking for a dish I'm sure my kids will love.

Over the years I have sampled many delicious dishes from many wonderful restaurants, homes, and faraway lands. When a dish teases my palate and leaves me begging for more, I make it my business to learn the how, what, where, and when about that particular recipe. I like to think with all the practice I get preparing and cooking these dishes, each one tastes better than the last. I haven't gotten one complaint yet!

I do hope you enjoy these recipes and the stories that accompany them, that help to explain what makes some so special to me, and what makes others as important as a family heirloom.

I can assure you that much time and effort—as well as love—has gone into all of the dishes I make or create. My sauce has been the subject of many Sunday dinner conversations with my relatives asking—no, begging—for my recipe, including the "secret ingredient" I intentionally leave out when running down the list of what goes into creating each large potful. I've even been approached about bottling and selling it.

I half expected to take my secrets with me, when the day comes that I hang up my oven mitts for good and go to that great kitchen in the sky. But then I remembered how frustrated I got each time I would beg Great Grandma or Mom for the ingredients of one of their popular, much raved about recipes. Therefore, I have decided to give away my secrets. Imitation is the sincerest form of flattery, they say, so if only a handful of you try to copy my sauces, pasta dishes, pizza recipes, and sweet and delicious desserts, I will be satisfied beyond belief.

What makes a dish even more delicious is the confidence that the cook or chef has before he or she even breaks an egg or butters a pan. It's not rocket science, ladies and gentlemen, but rather want and need. I cook because I *want* to show my loved ones how much I love them. I *need* to have an outlet to give back some of the joy they've given me so unselfishly over the years.

I hope all of you experience half as much joy as I have while sampling these delicious dishes. One thing to remember is to always make your list of necessary ingredients way before prep and cook time. There's nothing worse than running out of eggs or butter or some other easily stocked ingredient in the middle of preparing a recipe. Whatever preparation you can do ahead of time like peeling and cutting vegetables or garlic, should be done the day before you cook the recipe, as this will enable you to spend less time over a hot stove and more time at the table with your family and friends enjoying a meal made with love. Cooking is an art form in that most finished products are strategically placed and carefully arranged on plates for presentation. Following a recipe is so much more than just satisfying someone's hunger (a piece of bread can do that). Taking the time and effort to create a product that looks, feels, and tastes like a delicious work of art is equivalent to any artist painting a masterpiece. Anyone who thinks cooking is laborious and demeaning is missing out on doing a good deed for someone they love. Anyone who says cooking is old-fashioned and a thing of the past has no idea of the pleasures food can bring to the future. And anyone who feels cooking is not glamorous or sexy has no idea what a beautiful woman looks like—or what today's "modern man" is really looking for.

Mangia!

ITALY

Discovering the Motherland ∾

Believe it or not, my first trip to Italy was in 2005! I'm not exactly sure why I didn't make it my business to journey to the land of my ancestors before this. For some ridiculous reason I always equated a trip to Italy with work, and seeing as I was never much of a tourist, I never had the desire to book a flight on Al Italia. No kidding! Give me warm, sunny weather, a beach, some palm trees, a lounge chair, and a frozen piña colada any day—over donning comfortable shoes and trekking miles on foot with a tour guide from one historical point of interest to another.

Boy, was I in for a surprise! The minute I arrived in Rome on a hot, humid, and sunny day in June, having endured an uncomfortable seven and a half hour flight from New York (with no onboard movie and two predictable lousy meals), I was overcome by a serene and comforting aura. It might sound crazy, but the moment I stepped onto Italian soil, I felt like I was home—despite the fact I wasn't born in Italy and neither were my parents (nor their parents for that matter). The Italian people were incredibly helpful and warm—everywhere I turned people were approaching me, wanting to know if I needed help with my bags, or a ride to my hotel, or help with exchanging U.S. currency.

The trip was a last-minute itinerary—a new ad launch for my show, *Growing Up Gotti*. It was decided by the show's producers and show runner that we would shoot the entire third season in Italy. The producers were convinced the audience would flip for a chance to see my three sons and I research and explore our heritage. In fact, they were actually hoping we would find a few long-lost relatives and show up on their doorstep—on camera! The reality that we'd never been to Italy before would allow TV viewers to experience our excitement firsthand as well.

I can honestly say it was a soul-searching, nail-biting, and magnificently spine-tingling experience for me. It hit me as I was standing in the middle of St. Mark's Square in Venice, one of the most beautiful cities in the world, surrounded by culture, history, and tradition. My people, my ancestors, helped build such magnificent structures as the Coliseum, Trevi Fountain, and the Pantheon! It blew me away and left me with a strong sense of pride and gratitude. I was in awe of my surroundings, and feelings of nostalgia coursed through my veins. I spent three hours on the Internet researching my family tree. I even contacted a genealogy expert who told me my great grandfather Carmine Gotti came to America (via Ellis Island) in 1892 at the age of twenty-seven with his young bride Rose in tow and migrated to the Lower East Side of New York. Just learning this small piece of familial history hit me hard and nearly brought me to tears.

By the end of the first week in Italy, I had visited almost all of the notable historic sites in Rome: I attended mass at the Vatican, had a business meeting at St. Paul's Basilica, and even made three wishes and flipped three coins into Trevi Fountain.

I dined at the finest restaurants, visited the oldest local markets (where freshly hung and still warm mozzarella cheese was passed around to shoppers and tourists as a sign of hospitality and generosity), and became one with the local Italian residents. The word *gracious* didn't even begin to describe how warm and receptive they were to my sons and me.

As for the food, it was second-to-none! The appetizers were so good, I had to send back oversized portions for fear I would fill up before the main course. The pasta was so delicious I had second helpings at lunch and dinner. The meat cuts were tender enough to cut with a butter knife, and the homemade desserts were so rich and decadent I felt like I'd died and gone to heaven. Ordinary Italian delights and delicacies, like sliced buffalo mozzarella and tomato, or prosciutto and melon was so delicious I could've made a complete meal out of these "common" appetizers. The cheese was so . . . well . . . *cheesy*! The prosciutto was cured and sharp and it literally melted in your mouth. The cantaloupe was so fresh, juicy, and sweet it could've been served in place of dessert.

Which food is better tasting, Italian or Italian-American? Honestly, based on my own experience, I have to say Italian. While I was in Italy, I didn't have one bad meal! In fact, I actually looked forward to getting dressed up every afternoon and night and going to a restaurant—a task I hated and dreaded before Italy.

It didn't take long to realize what makes the Italian way of cooking taste better than the American version: passion! The Italians put much more passion and effort into each recipe. They prepare their dishes with pride and love for their friends and families—even those they've never met are considered "future friends." You get the point—the Italian people consider food and cooking an intimate act. It is an art form and much praise is given to those who can keep their family and friends satisfied with food.

In Italy, the *matriarch* of a family is shown much attention and adoration. In the United States, the American way of thinking puts the *patriarch* in the position of power, adoration, and respect. Most would call it macho and old-fashioned, but in truth, the Italians are by far much more old-fashioned than we are. In fact, Americans are considered way too "relaxed" and modern when it comes to their women; a matriarch's working outside of the home is not something that's common in Italy. A woman's place is in the kitchen (with her kids tied to her apron strings). The Italian woman doesn't take on an outside profession; rather, she is responsible for her family's welfare and well-being. Sewing a new suit of clothes, trying out new recipes, and keeping her family in a spotless and well-run household are her first priorities.

Some say the Americans' "too relaxed" way of thinking has more to do with a surge in divorce rates than anything else. Unfortunately, more and more American women are now forced to support their children in single-family households. Conversely, Italian women are less apt to seek a divorce. Turning a "blind eye" or a "deaf ear" to their husbands' indiscretions is common. The thought of having to first learn a worthy profession or trade for which they can be compensated while nearing middle age is not so appealing to these women.

On the other hand, Italian women are also celebrated for their efforts and credited with producing, nurturing, and caring for their broods like no other culture. As far as they are concerned, it is the highest honor to achieve matriarch status.

Luckily, some Italian-American men find a happy medium where tradition and position are concerned. It's called "having the best of both worlds." My father was one of them. While he was rigid in his beliefs that a woman's place was in the kitchen—that only a man worked outside the home—he also considered a woman who cared for her family in the proper manner a queen. There was no limit to his bragging when it came to my mother. As far as he was concerned, she was the "best cook in the world," watched and raised her children with a "mindful eye," could sew clothes better than some of the best-skilled tailors, and was also one of the most beautiful women in the world—"a younger Sophia Loren."

One of the most notable and unforgettable events during my trip to Italy was an impromptu cooking class given by a mother of six who looked, acted, and dressed every inch the traditional, Italian matriarch/cook. Five feet tall and weighing less than a hundred pounds, she wore a white smock and housedress much like the ones I remembered on

Mom and the other neighborhood ladies when I was growing up in downtown Brooklyn. Unlike most matriarchs in Italy, Anna is a modern woman; her husband is a CEO who travels back and forth between the United States and Italy. They have homes all over the world.

Much to my enjoyment, Anna, who'd been cooking professionally since she was eleven, allowed me to choose the entrée I most wanted to learn to cook. I chose one of my favorite dishes, linguine with white clam sauce. Up until that point, I'd ordered it four or five times while dining out for lunch and dinner, and each time it was better than the last! It was so delicious, I tried in vain to break it down into all the obvious ingredients in search of the exact steps for preparation—or some hundred-year-old "secret family recipe."

During my cooking lesson with Anna, I learned much about food: the origins of certain vegetables and fruits, the leanest cuts of meats, and what food combinations taste best. I learned the best prep methods as well as the fastest shortcuts. Most importantly, I learned that if you want to prepare a dish that will garner you raves, you should pay attention to details and not be afraid to roll up your sleeves and get your hands dirty. Also, you must use all fresh ingredients, even freshly made pasta.

While Anna prepared the dish I watched her every move. Was the secret ingredient some impossible-to-get delicacy? Or perhaps a difficult method of mixing the clam sauce before tossing it with the pasta noodles? No to all of the above. The so-called "secret" ingredient was nothing out of the ordinary at all. In fact, all the ingredients were basically the same ones I use every time I make linguine with white clam sauce. The "secret" ingredient was just a pinch more hard work—and a sprig of fresh basil. In Italy, all cooks believe the secret to a great plate of pasta depends on the cooking method in the end. Many Americans, myself included, use a basic step to finish making pasta: after straining the pasta, we pour on the sauce and mixed it at the table. But Italians mix the pasta into the sauce on the stovetop and cook it an additional 2 to 3 minutes to absorb the most flavor. Trust me, if you try this method once, you will *never* go back to the traditional way of straining pasta, then adding the sauce.

Do yourself a favor, take a lesson from the Italians: haste does indeed make bad taste . . . er . . . waste. Just by adding one additional step amounting to 5 extra minutes in the kitchen, I promise you, the dish you are preparing will be nothing short of *magnifico*!

1

SALADS
LETTUCE OPENERS

I've never really been a big salad lover—lettuce leaves seem better suited as a garnish than a delectable offering. Maybe it's because I grew up listening to my grandmother Della always complaining about waif-like women refusing to ingest "real" food, and opting instead to survive on low-calorie salads and tasteless raw veggies. Grandma was a good-looking woman in her heyday—her figure was akin to Sophia Loren's—and I don't remember her ever dieting.

"Real men like real woman," she'd say, "with a little meat on their bones, not skinny as a chicken!" And she's right—but still, a salad is a great opener for a sumptuous Italian meal, as every good cook knows. All of the salads in this section are delicious starters to meals so good you won't slow down until the last bit of dessert has been licked off the spoon and the dishes have been cleared!

ITALIAN TOMATO SALAD
Insalada di Pomorodi

SERVES 4 TO 6

½ head iceberg lettuce, sliced
lengthwise

3 firm beefsteak tomatoes, sliced
in eighths

1 cup pitted black olives

1 yellow onion, peeled and sliced
in eighths

1 peeled cucumber, cut into
½-inch rounds

½ cup virgin olive oil

½ cup balsamic vinegar

Salt and pepper to taste

1. In a large salad bowl, toss the lettuce, tomatoes, olives, onion, and cucumber slices.
2. In a glass jar, add the olive oil, vinegar, and salt and pepper. Cap the jar and shake vigorously until mixture is well blended.
3. Add half the oil and vinegar mixture to the salad bowl and toss four or five times. Then add the remaining oil and vinegar, and toss another four or five times.

The key to a great salad is keeping the greens and vegetables crisp and crunchy. Do not dress too early—five or ten minutes before mealtime is appropriate. Also, be consistent with your dressing ingredients, measuring them carefully: too much vinegar will give the salad a bitter taste, and too much oil lends a greasy taste.

TUSCAN BREAD SALAD
Panzanella

8 slices peasant bread (a mixture of any breads leftover or crusty—Italian, Tuscan, Ciabatta)

1 large red onion, diced

4 plum tomatoes, diced

1 cup red wine vinegar

¼ cup extra-virgin olive oil

Salt and black pepper to taste

1. Soak the bread in water briefly until it is soft, then gently squeeze it dry between paper towels.

2. Place the bread in a large bowl and add the onion, tomatoes, vinegar, oil, and salt and pepper. Using a spatula, stir the ingredients together until the bread disintegrates and the ingredients are evenly distributed.

3. Cover the bread salad and refrigerate for at least 1 hour before serving. Serve cold.

SALAD WITH FONTINA CHEESE AND PEARS

Insalata di Fontina e Pere   SERVES 4 TO 6

½ head iceberg lettuce

2 large pears, cored and sliced

½ cup olive oil

½ cup wine vinegar

6 ounces fontina cheese, cubed

Salt and pepper to taste

1. Wash the lettuce, and shred the leaves into a large salad bowl.
2. Add the pears, olive oil, vinegar, fontina cheese, and salt and pepper. Toss well and serve cold.

ARUGULA SALAD WITH ORANGES AND OLIVES

Insalata Rucola e Arranciata   SERVES 4 TO 6

12 ounces arugula

*3 seedless oranges, divided into
  natural sections*

4 ounces pitted black olives

Salt and pepper to taste

½ cup olive oil

3 tablespoons wine vinegar

1. Wash the arugula. Break the leaves in half, and place in a medium salad bowl.

2. Add the oranges, black olives, and salt and pepper, and toss to combine.

3. Add the olive oil and wine vinegar, tossing well again, and season with extra salt and pepper if needed.

CANTALOUPE AND ARUGULA SALAD

Insalata di Rucola e Melone   SERVES 4

10 ounces arugula   *1 cantaloupe*

Juice of 1 lemon   *Salt and pepper to taste*

¼ cup olive oil

1. Wash and drain the arugula. Chop the leaves into bite-size chunks, and place them in a salad bowl.
2. Drizzle the lemon juice and 2 tablespoons of the oil over the arugula leaves.
3. Using a melon baller, make round balls of melon and add to the arugula.
4. Drizzle the remaining 2 tablespoons olive oil over all, and season the salad with salt and pepper.

TOMATO, MOZZARELLA CHEESE, AND MIXED VEGETABLE SALAD

Insalata Caprese Condita

SERVES 4 TO 6

1 pound mozzarella cheese, cut
  into thick slices

7 large ripe tomatoes, sliced

2 carrots, chopped

2 celery stalks, chopped

1 onion, chopped

1 zucchini, cut into ¼-inch
  rounds

1 bell pepper, sliced

1 tablespoon capers

Salt and pepper to taste

½ cup olive oil

6 fresh basil leaves

1. Arrange the mozzarella slices side by side on a large platter. Arrange the tomato slices on top of the cheese.

2. Place the carrots, celery, onion, zucchini, and bell pepper in a medium mixing bowl, and add capers, salt and pepper, and oil. Toss this mixture well, until all the ingredients are coated with the oil.

3. Scoop the vegetable mixture over the tomatoes and mozzarella stacks, and garnish with basil leaves.

TRICOLOR SALAD WITH GOAT CHEESE

Insalada Tricolore Formaggio   SERVES 6

1 large bunch (about 12 ounces)
   arugula

1 medium head radicchio

2 medium heads endive

½ pound chévre or other goat
   cheese

2 medium tangerines (or
   mandarin oranges), peeled and
   sectioned

1 cup chopped walnuts

Raspberry Balsamic Vinaigrette
(recipe follows)

1. Wash the arugula and spread the leaves on paper towels to dry. Separate the radicchio and endive leaves, wash, and pat dry.

2. Arrange the arugula, radicchio, and endive in an attractive display on 6 salad plates. Place a teaspoon of goat cheese in the center of each and garnish with a tangerine slices. Sprinkle chopped walnuts onto each plate. Drizzle with Raspberry Balsamic Vinaigrette.

RASPBERRY BALSAMIC VINAIGRETTE

MAKES 1¾-2 CUPS DRESSING

½ cup fresh raspberries
½ cup extra-virgin olive oil
¾ cup balsamic vinegar

1. In a blender, purée the raspberries. Add the vinegar and continue blending.

2. With the blender on low, slowly pour the olive oil through the chute and process until the dressing is emulsified and looks smoothly blended.

3. Spoon lightly over individual salads.

2

PIZZAS

ITALY'S CROWN JEWEL

Let's face it—the Italians are known for many things but their cuisine is one of their biggest contributions to the world. Show me a person who doesn't know what a good slice of pizza tastes like, and I'll show you someone whose head's been in the sand!

I am a pizza fanatic! Give me any shape, style, size, or topping—I can devour a whole pie when I'm hungry. In Italy, the Italians consider pizza and pasta to be their culture's two most notable foods. Pizza is considered more a bread than a main dish. The Italians serve it at the beginning of almost every meal. Sometimes, it's called foccaccia or "pizza bread."

They don't see pizza the way we do—as a delicious and sinfully fattening lunch or dinner. Credit their love of tomatoes and bread with the invention of pizza. I found it most fascinating that pizza parlors are not rampant in Italy (yet in New York it seems like there's one on every corner). While we have two standard shapes, round and Sicilian (square), theirs are mostly rectangular and are simply referred to as "pizza."

BASIC PIZZA DOUGH

Impasto per Pizza

MAKES 1 12- TO 16-INCH PIZZA CRUST

¼ ounce fresh yeast or ¼ ounce (1 packet) active dry yeast

1 teaspoon sugar

⅔ cup lukewarm water (105° to 115°F)

3 cups unbleached white flour plus extra for kneading

1 teaspoon salt

2 tablespoons olive oil

1. Place the yeast in a small bowl along with the sugar and ⅓ cup of the lukewarm water. Stir the mixture slowly with a fork until the yeast dissolves, then set the mixture aside for 10 minutes. Stir once more just before using.

2. Place the flour in a mixing bowl and sprinkle the salt onto the flour. Make a hollow in the center of the flour mound, and pour in the yeast mixture along with the remaining ⅓ cup water and the olive oil.

3. Using a wooden spoon or your hands, fold the outer edges of the flour mound into the wet ingredients in the center, and stir well until the flour has evenly absorbed all the wetness and the dough holds its shape.

4. Transfer the dough to a lightly floured cutting board, and knead it by hand until it is smooth and elastic, or about 5 minutes. Sprinkle extra flour on your hands and the dough if it becomes too sticky to handle.

5. Place the dough into a lightly oiled bowl, and cover the bowl with cheesecloth. Let the dough rest until it doubles, about 1 hour. The time required for this varies by batch, but the dough is ready when it holds the impression of a finger poked into the center.

PIZZAS

I often save time by going to my local pizza parlor to grab a freshly prepared batch of pizza dough, but if you have the extra prep time, nothing beats a homemade pizza crust.

EGGPLANT PIZZA
Pizza con le Melanzane

SERVES 1 TO 2 (12- TO 16-INCH PIZZA)

1 recipe Basic Pizza Dough (page 20)

1 eggplant

¼ cup olive oil

Salt to taste

2 garlic cloves, minced

2 tablespoons finely chopped fresh parsley

One 8-ounce can crushed tomatoes, undrained

6 ounces mozzarella cheese, grated

8 fresh basil leaves, roughly chopped

Pepper to taste

1. Preheat the oven to 500°F.
2. Flour a cutting board or other flat surface, and use a rolling pin to roll the pizza dough into a round shape with a ¼-inch thickness.
3. Cut the eggplant into ¼-inch slices, and brush the slices lightly with 2 tablespoons of the olive oil.
4. Grill the eggplant slices for 3 to 4 minutes on a grill (or cook in a skillet with additional oil and turn frequently).
5. Sprinkle the grilled eggplant slices with salt, garlic, and parsley, and set aside.
6. Transfer the rolled-out dough to an oiled baking sheet or a pizza stone, and spread the tomatoes over top, leaving a 1-inch margin around the side. Sprinkle the mozzarella evenly over the tomato sauce. Drizzle with 1 tablespoon of olive oil.
7. Bake for 12 to 15 minutes, depending how you like your pizza.
8. Remove the pizza from the oven and place the eggplant slices on top of the melted cheese. Bake for an additional 5 minutes.
9. Remove the pizza from the oven, drizzle with the remaining 1 tablespoon oil and sprinkle the basil and pepper over the top.

WHITE PIZZA
Pizza Bianca

SERVES 1 TO 2 (12- TO 16-INCH PIZZA)

1 recipe Basic Pizza Dough (page 20)

1 tablespoon olive oil

4 ounces mozzarella cheese, grated

2 ounces Parmesan cheese, grated

Pepper to taste

6 fresh basil leaves, roughly chopped

1. Preheat the oven to 500°F.
2. Dust a cutting board and the palms of your hands with flour. Knead the pizza dough, and gather it into a ball. Using a rolling pin, roll the dough out to a ¼-inch thickness.
3. Oil a baking sheet and transfer the dough to the sheet, or use a pizza stone if you have one. Brush the dough with the olive oil and sprinkle the mozzarella and Parmesan cheeses evenly across the top. Sprinkle with pepper.
4. Bake for 12 to 15 minutes. When the pizza is cooked, sprinkle the top with basil and pepper to taste, and serve hot.

GARLIC PIZZA
Pizza con Aglio

SERVES 1 TO 2 (12- TO 16-INCH PIZZA)

1 recipe Basic Pizza Dough (page 20)

4 to 6 garlic cloves, minced

2 tablespoons dried oregano flakes

Salt and pepper to taste

3 tablespoons olive oil

1. Preheat the oven to 500°F.
2. Dust a cutting board and the palms of your hands with flour, and knead the pizza dough into a ball. Using a rolling pin, roll the dough out to a ¼-inch thickness.
3. Transfer the dough to an oiled baking sheet or a pizza stone, and sprinkle the garlic and oregano over the top.
4. Sprinkle the pizza with salt and pepper, and drizzle with 1 tablespoon of the olive oil.
5. Bake for 10 to 12 minutes, then drizzle with the remaining 2 tablespoons oil and serve hot.

PIZZA WITH ARUGULA AND MOZZARELLA

Pizza alla Rucola in Bianco   SERVES 1 TO 2 (12- TO 16-INCH PIZZA)

1 recipe Basic Pizza Dough (page 20)

Salt and pepper to taste

2 tablespoons olive oil

5 ounces mozzarella cheese, grated

3 ounces prosciutto

Handful of fresh arugula leaves

1. Preheat the oven to 450°F.
2. Dust a cutting board and the palms of your hands with flour.
3. Knead the pizza dough into a ball. Using a rolling pin, roll the dough out to a ¼-inch thickness on the cutting board.
4. Transfer the dough to an oiled baking sheet or pizza stone, and sprinkle with salt and pepper.
5. Brush the dough with 1 tablespoon of the olive oil and bake for 8 to 10 minutes, then sprinkle with mozzarella and bake for another 6 to 7 minutes.
6. Garnish the pizza with prosciutto and arugula, drizzle with the remaining 1 tablespoon oil, and serve.

PIZZA WITH BUFFALO MOZZARELLA, CHERRY TOMATOES, AND ZUCCHINI FLOWERS

Pizza al Fiori di Zucca   SERVES 1 TO 2 (12- TO 16-INCH PIZZA)

1 recipe Basic Pizza Dough (page 20)

1 tablespoon olive oil

Pepper to taste

6 ounces buffalo mozzarella, sliced

6 large zucchini flowers

10 cherry tomatoes

1. Preheat the oven to 500°F.
2. Dust a cutting board and the palms of your hands with flour. Knead the pizza dough, and gather it into a ball. Using a rolling pin, roll the dough out to a ¼-inch thickness.
3. Oil a baking sheet and transfer the dough to the sheet. Brush the dough with the olive oil, and sprinkle with pepper.
4. Lay the mozzarella slices on the pizza, and bake for 10 minutes.
5. Remove the pizza from the oven. Arrange the zucchini flowers and tomatoes on the pizza, and replace in the oven for an additional 5 to 7 minutes.

PIZZA WITH BLACK OLIVES
Pizza con le Olive Nere

SERVES 1 TO 2 (12- TO 16-INCH PIZZA)

1 recipe Basic Pizza Dough (page 20)

One 8-ounce can chopped tomatoes, undrained

10 to 12 black olives, pitted and sliced

2 teaspoons capers

3 tablespoons olive oil

1. Preheat the oven to 500°F.
2. Dust a cutting board and the palms of your hands with flour. Knead the pizza dough, and gather it into a ball. Using a rolling pin, roll the dough out to a ¼-inch thickness.
3. Transfer the dough to an oiled baking sheet or a pizza stone, and spread with the tomatoes and garnish with olives and capers.
4. Drizzle the dough with 1 tablespoon of the olive oil.
5. Bake for 15 minutes.
6. When the pizza is cooked, drizzle with the remaining 2 tablespoons oil.

3

APPETIZERS

THE WAY TO A MAN'S HEART
IS THROUGH HIS STOMACH

Forget what you've been told about what's attractive to men as far as women are concerned: big boobs, long legs, thick hair—or my personal favorite, a great personality. Ladies, I'm telling you, it's what you put in a man's stomach that will determine whether or not he'll spend Saturday nights with his poker buddies or plunk down beaucoup bucks for that 3½-carat sparkler and make an honest woman of you.

I have a friend I'll call Mr. Bachelor Man. He, like every other hot-blooded American man, admitted he would love to wake up next to a Pamela Anderson look-alike—but he also wants a woman who can cook. He even uses a slang world for watching beautiful women—appetizers! He says sitting with, talking to, and listening to a beautiful woman is like the warm-up for a delicious meal. Everyone knows a fulfilling five-course meal always begins with an appetizer, something Mr. Bachelor Man says he can't start any meal without. He said he gets "pretty excited watching a woman hard at work in the kitchen" (and he's not talking about her best Gypsy Rose Lee imitation—though something tells me that wouldn't hurt either).

One of the childhood memories I treasure is the look on Dad's face one day as he caught a glimpse of Mom racing around the kitchen trying to get Sunday dinner on the table. Well, his grin said it all.

Some women look at cooking as a necessary task in caring for their families—a job they feel goes unnoticed and unappreciated. That's be-

cause these women have been preparing meals as a chore *day after day—for decades—without receiving praise or any recognition.*

On the other hand, some women really enjoy practicing their culinary skills and view them as essentials of living like breathing or eating. They are so consumed with cooking, they look for excuses to sample new recipes and time-saving techniques. These women spend three quarters of their day in the kitchen and take their daily cooking regimes very seriously: preparing, baking, and arranging. They get an intense satisfaction from something as simple as a homemade loaf of bread: the satiny feel of the dough when kneaded, the smell of the yeast, or the delightful aroma of a freshly baked loaf. Even the phenomenon of a rising soufflé positively tickles them pink! These women dedicate themselves passionately and intimately to every culinary experience because they consider each recipe prepared for their family members or friends to be a labor of love.

One such woman is Marion Scotto, matriarch of the well-known Scotto restaurant family from New York City. Her family's flagship eatery, Fresco, is one of the city's most popular dining experiences, with an impressive client list of Italian-Americans such as James Gandolfini, Michael Imperioli, Sly Stallone, and Liza Minnelli. Celebrities as well as laypersons vie for reservations nightly because of the Scotto family's old-world style of Italian cooking. Marion Scotto and her family run the restaurant in a traditional hands-on fashion, and she makes every patron feel like part of her family.

Back in the early days, Dad made it his business to visit the Scotto restaurant at least three times a month (usually Wednesday nights) to feast on some of Mama Scotto's famous "peasant-style" dishes, like vinegared peppers and pork chops.

My father always bragged about how "dedicated, hardworking, and loyal" Mama Scotto is. Her loyalty to her family often amazed him. After starting out in the kitchen over twenty years ago, she still ran the Manhattan restaurant. Dad felt Marion was an icon for other Italian-American women, who could certainly "learn a thing or two" by taking notes from Mama Scotto. He believed today's women have too many amenities and shortcuts when it comes to cooking and caring for their families. He would often give me the speech about "how easy" we housewives and mothers have things today—"what with housekeepers and drive-through fast-food windows at McDonalds."

Whatever fondness my father had for Mama Scotto was definitely reciprocated. A few years ago, during a cooking segment to promote The Scotto Family Cookbook, Mama Scotto made an appearance on ABC's The View. The segment showcased Dad's favorite pork chops. Just before Mama Scotto pulled the delicious platter of meat out of the oven, she turned to the cameras and said, "I love preparing this dish so much, because it's a favorite of a dear friend of mine—a friend who at the moment is not well (Dad had recently been diagnosed with cancer). I pray for his recovery and thank God for the amazing strength he has to fight this."

In my opinion, there's nothing wrong with tradition and old-world style combined with living in New York, working in Manhattan, and mingling with Hollywood as my profession dictates. I, for one, enjoy a taste of the old days—when life was a heaping dose of simplicity and gourmet food was considered a luxury. Wishful thinking!

Ladies, forget trying so hard to be "thoroughly modern Millie," and embrace some old-fashioned traditions like cooking for your family. There's nothing degrading about spending time at the stove.

While we may not be able to turn the clock back—or convert such a fast-paced society to a simpler, more laid-back lifestyle—we can adopt some of the old-fashioned customs and traditions like learning to prepare a delicious feast, made with love, for our loved ones. The beauty of Italian women is that they are raised with many old-fashioned beliefs and traditions. They come from a culture that dictates traditional values. The notion that a young woman will grow up, marry, and take care of her home and household is common belief.

There's nothing unattractive about a woman who keeps a neat, well-organized home, and knows how to whip up a satisfying and hearty meal for her family. Besides, you might even get rewarded for your gracious hospitality come dessert time—like with a little extracurricular activity in the bedroom once the kiddies are asleep! Ladies, start with an appetizer—I doubt you'll be sorry.

Some "man-pleasing" recipes I've gotten the most response to are:

Fried Mozzarella (page 50)
Vegetable Risotto (page 92)
Italian-Style Broiled Steak (page 108)
Vinegared Peppers and Pork Chops (page 107)

BREAD FILLED WITH FRESH CHEESE

Focaccia con Formaggio Fresco

MAKES 1 FOCACCIA BREAD
(APPROXIMATELY 14 INCHES SQUARE)

¼ ounce (1 packet) dry yeast

1 teaspoon sugar

⅔ cup warm (105°–120°F) water

2 to 2½ cups flour

1 teaspoon salt

⅓ cup olive oil

10 ounces fresh mascarpone cheese

1. Put the yeast in a small bowl and add the sugar and ⅓ cup of the warm water. Whisk the ingredients with a fork until the yeast dissolves, then set the bowl aside for 15 minutes to allow the yeast to proof.

2. In a large mixing bowl, combine 2 cups of the flour, salt, yeast mixture, and remaining ⅓ cup water. Beat the ingredients together with an electric mixer on low until they become thick and doughy, and the mixture is smoothly combined. Add more flour if necessary.

3. Shape the dough into a ball and cover the surface lightly with olive oil. Set the ball in a large bowl, and cover with a damp cheesecloth. Set the covered bowl aside in a warm place for about 1½ hours, or until dough has approximately doubled in volume.

4. Preheat the oven to 500°F.

5. Dust a cutting board with flour, and transfer the dough to the board. Punch the raised dough and, with floured hands, knead it into a ball. Use a rolling pin to flatten the dough into a square of ¼-inch thickness.

6. Cut the flattened dough into two equal pieces.

7. Transfer half of the dough to an oiled baking sheet. Spread the mascarpone cheese over the surface of the dough, leaving a 1-inch border around edges.

8. Place the second dough piece on top of the cheese, and press the edges of the dough pieces together to form a seal. Using a fork, prick holes in the top of the dough surface and brush it with the remaining oil.

9. Bake the focaccia for 15 minutes, and serve warm.

OLIVE PASTE
Olivata

SERVES 6

12 ounces cured black olives, pitted and diced

½ cup olive oil

8 thin slices peasant-style bread (a mixture of any leftover bread—Italians HATE to waste!)

1 garlic clove, crushed

1. In a small mixing bowl, mix the diced olives with the olive oil until mixture is well blended. Cover the bowl and set aside.

2. Toast the bread on both sides until golden brown, and rub each slice with garlic.

3. Spread the bread pieces evenly with the olive mixture and serve at room temperature.

FRIED BREAD SQUARES
Quarti Fritto O Panzerotti

SERVES 6

½ tablespoon wet yeast, prepared
  according to package
  directions

1 cup warm water

2 cups flour

½ teaspoon salt

½ flour (for kneading)

2½ cups olive oil

Salt and pepper to taste

1. Dissolve the wet yeast in 1 cup of warm water.

2. Heap the flour in a large mixing bowl, and make a well in the center. Add the salt, wet yeast, and ½ cup of olive oil to the center of the well.

3. Mix the ingredients together with a spatula and then your hands, adding more water and flour until all of the dry mixture is absorbed into a rough dough.

4. Dust a wooden cutting board and your hands lightly with flour, and transfer the dough to the board. Knead the dough by hand until it is flat and smooth in consistency.

5. Roll the dough into a ball and place it in a large bowl that has been dusted with flour. Cover the bowl with a towel and let the dough rise for 2 hours.

6. Place the dough on a floured wooden board, and use a rolling pin to roll it out to a ½-inch thickness.

7. Cut the dough sheet into 3-inch squares.

8. In a large frying pan, heat the remaining 2 cups of olive oil. Deep-fry the squares until they are golden brown on both sides, and drain on double layer of paper towels. Can be served with fresh marinara sauce (recipe on page 129) or alone.

SOAKED BREAD AND TOMATOES

Pappa con il Pomodoro   SERVES 6 TO 8

½ cup olive oil

2 garlic cloves (chopped)

One 28-ounce can crushed
  tomatoes, undrained

2 to 3 fresh basil leaves

Salt and pepper to taste

2 cups chicken broth

1½ loaves stale Italian bread,
  thinly sliced

1. In a large frying skillet, heat the olive oil over medium heat and sauté the garlic until translucent.

2. Add the tomatoes, basil, and salt and pepper, and cover and cook for 15 minutes.

3. Add the chicken broth and bring the liquid to a boil, then add the bread slices and cook for another 15 minutes, stirring frequently.

4. Remove the skillet from the heat, and let the ingredients sit for 1 hour.

5. Stir the ingredients slowly but vigorously, until the bread disintegrates.

6. Serve the *pappa con il pomodoro* hot or lukewarm, adding a pinch more olive oil and a few more basil leaves. You may also add Parmesan cheese if you like, but I prefer not to—the basil and tomato flavor is superb alone!

Pappa con il pomodoro *is one of Italy's best appetizers, especially when served before pasta. The recipe is quite simple: like its name, it's nothing more elaborate than bread and tomatoes. Some folks* enjoy this dish in place of the more traditional breads served with dinner (like bruchetta).

"Sunday gravy bread dippers" love this dish, because it tastes so fresh and mimics a pot of gravy. Cooked tomatoes, spices, and Italian bread are all mixed together in a delicious sauce. I compliment the willpower of those who can limit themselves to an appetizer portion!

SWEET MELON WITH PROSCIUTTO

Prosciutto de Melone   SERVES 6 TO 8 AS A FIRST COURSE

1 honeydew or cantaloupe

½ pound thinly sliced prosciutto
  (lightly salted)

8 fresh basil leaves

1. Cut the melon in half and remove the seeds. Cut each half into quarters and remove the ripe flesh from melon skin, so that you have 8 slices total.

2. Place a strip of prosciutto across each melon slice. Garnish with 1 basil leaf per slice. Cover and chill until ready to serve.

STUFFED SWEET PEPPERS
Peperoni Ripieni al Forno   SERVES 6

½ cup olive oil

2 garlic cloves, minced

7 ounces ground beef

Salt and pepper to taste

2 eggs, lightly beaten

1 tablespoon capers

2 tablespoon grated pecorino
cheese

2 fresh basil leaves, shredded

6 red or green sweet bell peppers

½ teaspoon dried oregano

½ cup dry Italian bread crumbs

6 slices mozzarella cheese

1. Preheat the oven to 350° F.
2. Heat 5 tablespoons of the olive oil in a medium skillet over medium heat. Sauté the garlic, and add the ground beef when the garlic is translucent. Cover the skillet and cook for 5 minutes.
3. Add salt and pepper and remove the skillet from heat.
4. In a medium mixing bowl, combine the cooked meat, eggs, capers, pecorino cheese, and basil, mixing well.
5. Cut the tops off the peppers and remove the seeds. Set aside the tops.
6. Stuff each pepper with the meat mixture and sprinkle with oregano and bread crumbs. Put one slice of mozzarella on top of each pepper and cover with the pepper tops.
7. In a large casserole pan, spread the remaining 3 tablespoons olive oil, then place stuffed peppers in the pan and bake for 40 minutes.

STUFFED MUSHROOMS
Teste di funghi Ripiene

SERVES 6

½ cup extra-virgin olive oil

2 dozen large white mushrooms, stems removed

1 cup seasoned Italian bread crumbs

1 garlic clove, minced

1½ teaspoons chopped fresh Italian parsley

2 tablespoons grated Parmesan cheese

Salt and pepper to taste

¼ cup dry white wine

1. Preheat the oven to 350°F.
2. Grease a large baking sheet with 3 tablespoons of the olive oil. Clean the mushrooms well and arrange them, centers up, on the baking sheet.
3. In a medium mixing bowl, combine the bread crumbs, garlic, remaining 5 tablespoons oil, the parsley, grated cheese, salt and pepper, and white wine, and mix well. The mixture should be pasty.
4. Spoon equal portions of the mixture into the center of each mushroom, sprinkling with additional grated cheese if desired.
5. Cover the mushrooms with foil and bake for 12 minutes. Remove the foil and continue baking for an additional 3 minutes. Serve hot.

SAUTÉED MUSHROOMS

SERVES 6

½ cup extra-virgin olive oil

2 garlic cloves, minced

1½ pounds fresh white cap
mushrooms, sliced

½ cup dry white wine

Salt and pepper to taste

2 tablespoons chopped fresh
Italian parsley

1. Heat the oil in a medium skillet over medium heat. Add the garlic and sauté until golden. Remove and discard the garlic.
2. Add the mushrooms and sauté for 6 to 7 minutes, or until tender.
3. Add the wine, and salt and pepper. Bring the liquid to a boil and cook for 2 minutes.
4. Remove the skillet from heat and stir in the parsley, and serve hot.

ROASTED PEPPERS
Peperoni Arrostiti

SERVES 4 TO 6 AS AN APPETIZER

6 red bell peppers

3 yellow bell peppers

½ cup extra-virgin olive oil

1 tablespoon raisins (optional)

2 tablespoons pine nuts

1 garlic clove, minced

1 teaspoon chopped fresh Italian parsley

Salt and pepper to taste

1. Preheat the broiler.
2. Cut the tops off the peppers. Clean out the seeds and veins. Cut the peppers lengthwise into 1-inch strips.
3. Lay the pepper slices on a cookie sheet, skin side up. Broil 6–10 minutes, turning once, until skin is slightly charred. Remove the pepper slices from broiler and immediately put into a large brown paper bag. Seal the bag tightly (this allows peppers to steam) for about 20 minutes.
4. Remove the peppers from bag and peel off the charred skin. Place the strips in a strainer over a flat dish for at least 2 hours.
5. In a bowl, combine the peppers, oil, raisins (if desired), nuts, garlic, and parsley. Add salt and pepper. Allow the peppers to marinate for at least 1 to 2 hours before serving.

STUFFED ARTICHOKES
Carciofi Ripiene

SERVES 6 AS A SIDE DISH
OR 12 AS AN APPETIZER (CUT IN HALVES)

6 large artichokes

1 lemon, halved

1 cup lemon juice

1½ cups seasoned Italian bread
   crumbs

½ cup grated Parmesan cheese

1 garlic clove, crushed

1½ tablespoons chopped fresh
   Italian parsley

Salt and pepper to taste

1 cup extra-virgin olive oil

1. Preheat the oven to 350°F.
2. Wash the artichokes in cold water.
3. Squeeze the juice of ½ lemon into a large bowl of cold water and set aside.
4. Remove the stalks from the ends of the artichokes and pluck off the rough outer leaves. With a sharp knife or kitchen shears, cut the artichoke across the top to remove the sharp spikes.
5. Turn the artichokes upside down on a countertop or cutting board, and press down and roll the artichokes to cause the entire flower to open up. As each artichoke is opened, place it into the bowl of water with lemon juice.
6. In a medium mixing bowl, combine the bread crumbs, cheese, garlic, parsley, and salt and pepper. Set aside.
7. Remove the artichokes from the lemon water, and place them face down on a double layer of paper towels. Allow the artichokes to dry (approximately 15 minutes).
8. When the artichokes are dry, place an equal portion of the bread crumb mixture between every leaf of each artichoke, including the

centers. Set the artichokes upright (stem-side down) in a medium roasting pan that has been filled with 1 inch of water, with 1 tablespoon salt and ½ cup of the olive oil.

9. Drizzle the remaining ½ cup oil over artichokes in the pan. Cover the pan and simmer over high heat for approximately 15 minutes.

10. Squeeze the juice of ½ lemon over all the artichokes, then place lemon halves in the bottom of the pan. Cover again and place the pan in the oven. Cook for 10 minutes.

These make a great appetizer when cut in halves.

CARPACCIO

SERVES 4 TO 6 IN APPETIZER PORTIONS

3 tablespoons lemon juice

10 ounces beef sirloin, sliced very thin

4 white mushrooms, sliced thin

3 tablespoons olive oil

Salt to taste

1 tablespoon freshly ground black pepper

1. Spritz a medium-size platter with 1 tablespoon of the lemon juice.
2. Arrange the beef on a large platter, spacing each slice evenly.
3. Scatter the mushrooms over the meat slices.
4. Whisk together 3 tablespoons of the olive oil, the remaining 2 tablespoons lemon juice, salt, and the pepper in a medium bowl.
5. Spoon the dressing evenly over the beef slices.

Carpaccio is absolutely delicious, but before you eat it you should remember that eating any raw meat increases your risk of ingesting foodborne bacteria. That said, be sure you and your butcher treat your beef sirloin accordingly.

PASTA AND BEANS
Pasta e Fagioli   SERVES 6

12 ounces dried cannellini beans

¼ cup virgin olive oil

1 white onion, chopped

1½ cups baby carrots

1 cup chopped celery

2 garlic cloves, chopped

2 fresh basil leaves

One 28-ounce can crushed
  tomatoes, undrained

1 cup chicken broth

Salt and pepper to taste

1 pound fresh ditalini pasta

½ cup freshly grated Parmesan
  cheese

1. Soak the beans overnight. When ready to use, boil briefly in salted water, then drain and set aside.

2. In a large skillet, heat the oil over medium heat.

3. Sauté the onion for 1 minute, and then add the carrots, celery, garlic, and basil leaves. Cover the skillet and cook for 12 minutes.

4. Add the tomatoes, chicken broth, beans, and salt and pepper. Cover the skillet and simmer for an additional 40 minutes.

5. Fill a large pot with water and bring to a rolling boil. Add the pasta and cook for approximately 6 minutes, or until al denté.

6. Drain the pasta and add it to the tomato mixture. Cover the skillet and cook for an additional 2 to 3 minutes.

7. Transfer the *pasta e fagioli* to a large serving bowl or platter, and garnish with the Parmesan cheese.

CHOPPED TOMATOES ON CRUSTY BREAD SLICES

Baby Bruschettas

MAKES ABOUT 12 PIECES

½ cup balsamic vinegar

½ cup virgin olive oil

Salt and pepper to taste

6 sprigs fresh parsley

6 sprigs fresh basil

3 beefsteak tomatoes, chopped

One 1-pound loaf stale (1- or 2-day-old) Italian bread, uncut

1. Place the vinegar, olive oil, salt and pepper, 2 sprigs of the parsley, and 2 sprigs of the basil in a jar with a lid. Close the jar and shake vigorously for 1 minute.
2. Place the tomatoes in a medium mixing bowl, and add the vinegar mixture. Toss the ingredients to combine them, and let chill in the refrigerator for 30 minutes.
3. Cut the Italian bread lengthwise.
4. Lay the bread crust-side down, and toast the bread under a broiler for 1 minute, or until golden brown.
5. Spoon the tomato mixture evenly over the pieces of toasted bread.
6. Chop up remaining 4 sprigs of parsley and basil and evenly distribute as garnish on top of the *bruschetta*.

You can prepare the elements of this appetizer ahead of time. But bruschetta will become soggy if left to sit too long. The tomato mixture should be spooned onto the bread just minutes before serving.

MOZZARELLA, TOMATO, AND BASIL SLICES WITH BALSAMIC DRIZZLE

Insalata Caprese Classica   SERVES 6

2 firm beefsteak tomatoes cut
   into 6 slices each

6 slices fresh mozzarella (lightly
   salted preferred)

6 fresh basil leaves

Salt and pepper to taste

½ cup extra-virgin olive oil

½ cup balsamic vinegar

1. Arrange the tomato slices on a flat platter. Place 1 mozzarella slice on top of each tomato slice, then garnish each with a basil leaf.

2. Sprinkle each stack with salt and pepper to taste.

3. Whisk the olive oil and vinegar together in a separate bowl, and drizzle over each mozzarella and tomato stack.

4. Cover the platter with plastic wrap and chill until you are ready to serve.

FRIED MOZZARELLA
Mozzarella in Carrozza

SERVES 6

Six ½-inch slices fresh mozzarella

6 slices white bread, crusts
   trimmed off

1 cup flour

2 eggs, beaten

2 cups seasoned dry bread
   crumbs

2½ tablespoons chopped fresh
   parsley

5 cups vegetable oil

1. Lay a slice of mozzarella on top of each slice of bread. Cut the bread and cheese stacks in half.

2. Put the flour in a shallow bowl or plate. Lay each stack of bread and cheese in the flour and coat both sides, shaking off the excess. Set aside.

3. Put the beaten eggs into a bowl. In a separate bowl, mix the bread crumbs and the parsley.

4. Dip each floured bread and cheese stack in the eggs, then lay it in bread crumbs, taking care to coat both sides well. Shake off any excess crumbs and set the stacks aside until you are ready to fry them.

5. Heat the vegetable oil over medium heat in a medium-size saucepan.

6. When the oil is hot, fry the mozzarella and bread stacks for approximately 1 minute on each side, or until the bread crumbs have browned. You can fry three or four stacks at once, but don't overcrowd the saucepan. Remove the stacks from the oil with a slotted spoon or fork, and lay them on a double layer of paper towels to drain.

7. Preheat the oven broiler.

8. Arrange the bread stacks on a cookie sheet. Place the sheet under the broiler on the top rack for a total of 40 seconds (20 seconds per side), flipping once.

9. Transfer the finished appetizers to a flat platter, and serve with warm marinara sauce, either by pouring the sauce on top or serving in a bowl for dipping.

EGGPLANT APPETIZER
Caponata

SERVES 6

½ cup olive oil

1 garlic clove (chopped)

2 white onions, chopped

2 bell peppers, seeds removed
and thinly sliced

1 pound Italian plum tomatoes,
tops and seeds removed

1 pound zucchini, thinly sliced

2 eggplants, cleaned, peeled, and
cubed

Salt and pepper to taste

1. Heat ¼ cup of the olive oil in a medium saucepan. Add the garlic, onions, bell peppers, tomatoes, zucchini, and eggplants.

2. Sauté all the vegetables over high heat, and season with salt and pepper. Lower the heat and let the vegetables simmer in their own juices for 20 minutes.

3. Add the remaining ¼ cup of oil, and cover and cook for an additional 10 minutes. Remove the pan from heat, and serve hot.

Caponata *is an Italian dish that originated in Sicily. It's a very flavorful appetizer used in place of dips, sauces, and salads. There are many recipes use* caponata *as a base: chicken* caponata, caponata *toast, eggs* caponata, *and pasta* caponata *are just a few.* Caponata *is delicious and filling, yet light; it can even be used as a meal itself. Most people who taste* caponata *tell me you can never "just sample one bite!"*

4 ❦

PASTA

MACARONI IN MINK

Food has long been associated with emotions—good and bad—as a means of comfort for anxiety, nervousness, and stress. Women, in particular, eat when they are depressed, and starve when they are happy. In most cases of failed romance, women seem to bond together—as in the recent case of my good pal, whom I'll call "Lela"—a gorgeous A-list actress who seemed to have everything except the man she loved. Lela was one of those women you can't help but hate: she's beautiful, smart, comes from a wealthy family, and pretty much can have any guy she wants—any guy except her ex-fiancé, whom I'll call Louis. Her story is far from unique, but definitely worth telling. There are millions of Lelas in this world—women who live their lives by the seat of their pants. We've heard the story numerous times as well: boy meets girl, boy gets girl, boy no longer wants girl. While it's heart wrenching and depressing, it's also reality. So, I'm taking the liberty of including a scene out of Lela's life in my cookbook because it offers inspiration and hope to a multitude of women still waiting for their chance at happiness.

Lela arrived last—it was nearly 9 P.M. when she burst through the door of Kate's classic six-room apartment on Park Avenue. Aside from her flustered expression Lela looked absolutely divine, positively glowing with her honey-colored, precisely cut, shiny bob and expertly applied smoky nighttime makeup. She bounced about the kitchen swinging numerous shopping bags through the air.

"I did an awful lot of damage today at the four Bs [Barneys, Bergdorf's, Bendel's, and Bloomingdale's]. I bought this incredibly sexy pale pink

La Perla teddy and matching tap pants." Lela rummaged through the dark purple bag from Bergdorf's.

"And I just had to have the new Jimmy Choo flats. The salesgirl had a pair on hold for me she'd hidden in the back as soon as the shipment arrived. I always say 'it's who you know' that counts."

As Lela continued showing off her wares—even modeling a cream-colored sheath that, in her words, she'd "practically stolen"—the rest of us stared in disbelief, even scratching our heads. Wasn't it just last night Lela had announced in her most dire voice she'd been left at the altar by a "no good, two-timing cheat with cold feet"? Wasn't it just this morning she'd called the three of us to announce she was convinced she was "having a breakdown"—something about a "broken heart" and blah, blah, blah, not to mention the grief and guilt she got from her parents for spending nearly $300,000 from her trust fund to pay for the elaborate, over-the-top, Donald and Melania Trump–style wedding?

This morning we had an emergency conference call to discuss the evening's plans—usually, on Thursday nights the four of us get together for what we called "ladies pasta night out." With hundreds of hours of diaper changes, late-night feedings, menu planning, grocery shopping, housekeeping, doctor visits, after-school activities, and countless car pools, we were all too eager to arrange for the sitter, slip into our Manolos, and race for the front door like bats out of hell! Judging by our excitement, you'd think we were racing to some hot, new, much hyped, underground club to sip Cristal while sitting at George Clooney's table. Instead we took turns picking a favorite Italian restaurant or sometimes we alternated hosting these dinners at our homes and together we would prepare pasta fit for a king, sure to bring on hours of gossip and laughter. Hey, it may not exactly be Paris Hilton's idea of a wild night out, but it worked for us! It was our only escape—a nighttime pass to remember just how "footloose and fancy-free" we all were in our youth.

It was Kate's turn to entertain the ladies, and if the delightful aroma permeating the apartment was any indication of that night's meal, we were in for a delicious feast. She had prepared macaroni and meatballs, buttered baby carrots, and creamy mashed potatoes; Italian lettuce salad; orecchiette pasta with broccoli rabe and sausage; and for dessert, homemade cannolis filled with ricotta cheese cream, and lemon gelato.

"I am sooo exhausted—in a good way, mind you." Lela continued. "It all began with a late morning trip to Bloomies to pick up a pair of black pumps for Celia's wedding Saturday—a simple errand that turned into a major shopping spree!" Lela smiled from ear to ear and she looked positively radiant—a far cry from the wreck she was last night.

The new Lela was definitely impressive, but the suspense was absolutely killing me, so I blurted out, "What happened to your broken heart? Just hours ago you were crying over Louis."

"Louis who?" Lela laughed.

"I had the best day shopping—and I owe it all to a beautiful and charming salesgirl at Barneys."

Now we were all completely confused. I waited for someone else to break the silence, but when no one else spoke I said, "Lela, what could a salesgirl possibly do to change your desperate and depressed mood? Besides show you the new Jimmy Choo fall collection, that is."

A radiant Lela replied, "Well, I was in the lingerie department checking out the new Nicole Miller line when I lost it—I was thinking about the honeymoon to Rome Louis and I were supposed to take. I imagined him walking through the Coliseum, Trevi Fountain, and the Basilica with some twenty-year-old supermodel. I had a full-on pity party. I was crying, shaking, a real wreck. I just couldn't stop thinking about how happy we were supposed to be." Lela continued giving us details about different fantasies she'd planned for their romantic honeymoon: how Italy was Louis's favorite place on Earth, the gondola ride they would take their first night in Venice—and on and on.

Now, I was really confused. Perhaps she and Louis had managed to work things out. Perhaps he'd called her when she was at Barneys and told her he was a fool to call off the wedding—that he really did love her. Maybe he added a million "I'm sorrys" and a promise to "make things up to her."

Boy, was I wrong!

"This beautiful salesgirl noticed me crying and pulled me into a back dressing area. She handed me a box of Kleenex then told me her story—how she'd married her high school sweetheart and was the happiest girl in the world."

Then Lela's expression turned glum.

"One week after their honeymoon she started getting anonymous phone calls from a woman who always said the same thing, 'He loves me. He wants me. We are going to be together forever.'"

Lela grew much more animated now, rising from her seat and walking over to the Garland stove in the center of the kitchen.

"One month to the day they were married, she found out she was pregnant. It should have been the second happiest day of her life!"

"But . . ."

A very impatient Rachel interrupted. "Lela, finish the story—the suspense is killing me!"

"Okay, okay," *Lela continued.* "That night she prepared a special romantic dinner for her husband. She decided she would tell him about the baby over his favorite meal of beef Wellington and mashed potatoes. He was expected home at 8:00. Unfortunately, his girlfriend of three years rang the bell at 7:15!"

All mouths dropped. Rachel seemed the most disappointed. She covered her mouth and managed to blurt out, "Oh, my God!"

Lela bit down on her lower lip, then continued.

"Oh yes! And boy, did she give Wifey an earful! She'd been sleeping with her husband since her senior year of high school. They met at a party for a mutual friend, they hooked up, and had been together ever since, meeting every Thursday night, right up until that day!"

I was still in shock—and couldn't find the right words after this bombshell of a story—but by the way Lela grew even more animated, I could tell things were about to get even juicier!

"What did the wife do? Did she freak? Of course she freaked!"

Rachel seemed so consumed one would think she knew the unlucky couple. She was eager for more details, begging Lela to continue between bites of baby bruschetta.

Then, as promised, Lela delivered the perfect Hollywood ending.

"Wifey managed to get rid of the hussy—but not before getting her phone number and promising to call later to finish their discussion. The moment the door closed behind the other woman, Wifey raced around the kitchen putting together her plan of revenge."

"Oh my God! The suspense is killing me," Rachel squealed. "Please tell me! Tell me!"

The storyteller inside me was convinced Lela would deliver a worthy climax. At the moment she held center stage and was rather enjoying her fifteen minutes of fame, so to speak. Besides, just this morning Lela was suicidal—tonight she was as overjoyed as a ballerina on a balcony, her gleeful eyes dancing around the room.

"Wifey poisoned him!" Lela deadpanned.

The room fell so silent you could hear a pin drop. While it wasn't exactly the ending we expected, everyone's reaction spoke volumes. Expressions of disbelief and relief spread around the banquet-size table—especially relief, that Lela was no longer depressed and headed for a breakdown. Whatever prompted Lela's sudden mood change and removed her from a "revenge-induced suicide watch" was okay by all of us—even if it was at some unfortunate hubby's expense . . . er . . . demise. As most women already know, we gals rarely suffer solo—a breakup is generally a shared tragic event. A nail-biting night of crying, chocolate bingeing, and revenge plotting requires group involvement. After hearing about the meeting, courtship, and progress of a best friend's new guy, every day, a million times over, whatever happens in the end affects all of us as if we were the woman wronged! It's called FMC (female misery camaraderie)—and while no one in the room dared say it, we were all over the moon with joy that Lela was no longer broken-hearted and seeking revenge.

"Oh, don't look at me with such confused faces—the bastard didn't die. Wifey added a heaping dose of ipecac syrup to his pasta sauce and a pinch of laxative to his meatballs—he had it coming out of both ends well into the wee hours of the morning!"

The girls and I broke out into a wave of harmonious laughter; tears were streaming down our faces. It was the best tale of romantic revenge we had ever heard; we spent the next ten minutes complimenting Wifey on a job well done. No matter that we didn't know her—for the moment she represented the wronged woman in all of us. And while none of us were savvy enough to pull off such a successful plan of revenge at the time we were wronged, we all filed the knowledge under "F" for any future bastard who even thinks about it!

Unfortunately, we were so deep in gleeful thought that no one smelled the biscuits burning in the oven! By the time the smoke alarm sounded, the room was covered in a thick, choking haze. One of us ran for the windows, while another opened the front door. Lela panicked and doused water on the cookie pan now filled with charred hockey pucks. In seconds, the entire kitchen became a disaster area! Smoke, water, and pieces of black overcooked dough were splattered everywhere—on the countertops, table, floor, and even the ceiling. Our carefully planned and prepared dinner of macaroni and meatballs was ruined. But somehow it didn't matter. Sure, we were all starving and craving a good meal, but Lela's bounce back from the brink was all that seemed important in the end. That and the wise advice we were all given by a wife none of us knew (advice I'm sure will come in handy in the future). Oh, and did I mention the great-looking, buff firemen that stormed the apartment? Ironically, Lela lost her footing and slipped on the wet marble and needed some assistance. A gorgeous, sandy-haired captain scooped her off the floor and carried her to safety—and being the dutiful public servant that he was, he insisted on escorting Lela home that night, even helped her on with her coat, a brand new, full length, Blackglama mink.

"Hey," Lela explained (before running off with her prince . . . er . . . fireman), "it caught my eye at Bergdorf's, and hearing Wifey's sad story made me realize I have much to be thankful for. So, the moment Wifey *said goodbye, I headed straight for the fur department and picked out the most expensive mink I could find."*

While I was delighted Lela was happy, I couldn't help thinking about the grief she'd gotten from her parents because she'd dipped so deeply into her trust fund to pay for the wedding that never would be. I thought about reminding Lela to curb her spending impulses—at least for a little while. Boy, was I glad I hadn't when she announced, "Luckily, I still have one or two credit cards with Louis's name on them. You can't imagine the expression on my face when I told the salesgirl to charge the mink to him!"

Lela smiled from ear to ear when she said, "And I can't think of a better way to get revenge than to sit with my best friends, eating macaroni-in-mink."

RIGATONI PASTA WITH TOMATO SAUCE
Pasta Filetto di Pomodoro

SERVES 4

½ cup olive oil

4 ounces prosciutto, chopped

1 cup chopped onion

One 28-ounce can crushed
   tomatoes, undrained

Salt to taste

½ teaspoon dried oregano

Black pepper to taste

7 fresh basil leaves

1½ tablespoons chopped fresh
   parsley

1 pound rigatoni pasta

Parmesan cheese for garnish

1. In a large saucepan, heat the oil over medium heat. Add the proscuitto and onion, and sauté for 5 to 6 minutes.

2. Add the tomatoes to the pot and bring the mixture to a boil. Reduce the heat and let the contents simmer covered for 30 minutes.

3. Add the salt, oregano, pepper, basil, and parsley, and cook for another 10 minutes.

4. Cook the rigatoni according to package directions. When the pasta is al denté, drain it and return it to the pot. Add 2 cups of the simmering tomato sauce and cook for 3 minutes, stirring constantly.

5. Transfer the pasta to a serving dish and spoon the remaining sauce over the pasta. Garnish with Parmesan cheese to taste.

HOMEMADE FETTUCCINE PASTA

SERVES 4 (1 POUND)

3 cups flour
½ teaspoon salt

3 eggs

1. Sift flour and salt into a mound on a cutting board or a clean, flat surface.
2. Make a hollow in the center of the mound and break the eggs into it. Using a whisk or fork, gently whip the eggs into the flour until all the flour is mixed in.
3. The dough will thicken as the eggs are absorbed. Using your hands, shape the dough into a ball. Knead the dough thoroughly, then fold it in half and continue to knead.
4. Set the dough aside for 20 to 25 minutes.
5. Transfer the dough to a lightly floured cutting board, and, using a rolling pin, roll the dough out to a ¼-inch thickness. With a wet knife, cut the dough into long strips, roughly ½ inch wide, or use a pasta machine for precise shaping.
6. Cook the pasta according to the recipe specifications.

Nothing improves a delicious pasta recipe better than homemade noodles. There's a distinct freshness that homemade pasta brings to any recipe. In Italy, you'll rarely find a restaurant that serves dried pasta: fresh pasta is as accessible as a slice of pizza! Sure, it takes increased effort on the cook's part, but you know what they say: "It's the things in life that come hardest that are the most enjoyable."

LINGUINE WITH PEAS AND PROSCIUTTO

Linguine con Prosciutto e Piselli   SERVES 6

½ cup virgin olive oil

1 onion, finely chopped

½ cup finely chopped prosciutto

1 chicken bouillon cube

1 cup hot water

One 8-ounce can peas, drained

Salt and pepper to taste

1 pound linguine

1. In a large skillet over medium, heat the oil, then sauté the onion until translucent.
2. Stir in the prosciutto and sauté for an additional 3 minutes.
3. Dissolve the chicken bouillion in the hot water, and add it to the skillet along with the peas and salt and pepper. Cover and cook for 5 minutes.
4. In a medium pot, boil water and add the linguine. Cook until al denté, 6 to 8 minutes.
5. Drain the pasta, and add the pasta to the peas and prosciutto in the skillet. Cook for an additional minute, tossing often, and serve hot.

SEMOLINA GNOCCHI

Gnocchi di Semolino   SERVES 4 AS A MAIN DISH OR 8 AS AN APPETIZER

1 cup water

4 cups whole milk

1 tablespoon salt

1½ sticks unsalted butter, cut into 1-tablespoon pats

½ pound semolina

¼ cup freshly grated Parmesan cheese

1. Preheat the oven to 350°F.

2. Pour the water and milk into a large pasta pot, then add the salt and 1 stick of the butter. Bring the mixture to a boil over medium heat.

3. Pour the semolina into the boiling liquid, whisking continuously to prevent lumps from forming. Cook the semolina for 3 minutes, until the mixture is thick.

4. Spoon the semolina onto a damp cutting board and use a spatula to spread it evenly to a ¼-inch thickness. Allow the seminola to cool and harden.

5. Cut the semolina into 2-inch squares, and place the squares on a non-stick baking pan. Dust the squares with Parmesan cheese, dot with the remaining ½ stick butter, and bake for 10 minutes, or until the tops are lightly golden. Remove the semolina gnocchi from the oven and serve immediately. This dish goes well with lamb or a tomato sauce. *Note:* Refrigerate leftover gnocchi immediately.

BASIC POTATO GNOCCHI
Gnocchi (Patata)   SERVES 4 TO 6

1½ pounds potatoes, peeled and   2 eggs
*   cubed   2 cups flour*

1. Boil the potato cubes in a large pot for approximately 30 minutes.
2. Drain the potatoes, and transfer to a large bowl. Mash the potatoes until there are no large lumps remaining. Add the eggs and flour, and mix well with a wooden spoon.
3. Transfer the mixture to a lightly floured cutting board, and knead by hand until smooth and soft, or for about 5 minutes. The dough should be slightly sticky, but add more flour if it becomes too sticky to work with.
4. Divide the mixture into 6 or 7 equal pieces. Roll each section into a log about ½ inch wide and 12 inches long.
5. Cut each log into pieces about 1 inch long, and use a fork to give the gnocchi decorative grooves around the circumference, if so desired.
6. Cook the gnocchi in a large pot of boiling water for about 4 minutes, and add sauce as desired.

GNOCCHI WITH BUTTER AND PARMESAN CHEESE

Gnocchi di Cuneo

1 pound Basic Potato Gnocchi (page 64)

¼ cup unsalted butter

½ cup grated or cubed Parmesan cheese

Salt and pepper to taste

1. Add the gnocchi to a large pot of boiling water and cook for 4 minutes. Drain the gnocchi and set aside.

2. In a medium saucepan over low heat, melt the butter and add the Parmesan cheese. Add salt and pepper, and stir while the cheese melts.

3. Add the gnocchi to the melted butter and cheese. Cook over low heat for 2 minutes, stirring frequently to combine all the ingredients, and serve immediately.

POTATO PASTA WITH GORGONZOLA AND TOMATO SAUCE

Gnocchi al Gorgonzola e Pomodoro   SERVES 6

1 pound Basic Potato Gnocchi
  (page 64)

¼ cup unsalted butter

7 ounces Gorgonzola cheese,
  crumbled

One 28-ounce can crushed
  tomatoes, undrained

Salt and pepper to taste

⅓ cup freshly grated Pecorino
  Romano

1. In a large pot of boiling water, cook the gnocchi for 4 minutes. Drain thoroughly and set aside.

2. In a large deep skillet over medium-high heat, melt the butter and add the Gorgonzola.

3. When the cheese is melted, add the tomatoes and salt and pepper. Stir well to mix the ingredients, then reduce the heat to low. Cover the skillet and simmer for approximately 30 minutes.

4. Add the gnocchi to the simmering sauce. Stir to distribute the gnocchi through the sauce, and cook for an additional 2 minutes.

5. Toss the gnocchi and tomato sauce well. Transfer to a large platter and sprinkle with Pecorino Romano. Toss well again and serve immediately.

FUSILLI WITH BELL PEPPERS
Fusilli con Peperoni

SERVES 6

1 pound fresh fusilli pasta

¼ cup olive oil

3 garlic cloves, minced

2 red bell peppers, seeds removed and thinly sliced

2 yellow peppers, seeds removed and thinly sliced

6 fresh basil leaves

Salt and pepper to taste

1. Add the pasta to a large pot of boiling water, and cook the fusilli until al denté, 6 to 8 minutes. Drain the pasta and set aside.

2. In a medium skillet, heat the olive oil over low heat. Sauté the garlic and peppers for 10 minutes, or until the peppers have a soft and mushy consistency. Add the basil leaves and salt and pepper. Cover the skillet, and let simmer for an additional 10 minutes.

3. Add the pasta to the skillet, tossing well. Cook over low heat for an additional 2 to 3 minutes. Transfer the pasta to a large serving platter and serve hot.

NEAPOLITAN-STYLE FUSILLI
Fusilli alla Napolitana

SERVES 4

½ cup olive oil

One 28-ounce can crushed tomatoes, undrained

1 tablespoons chopped fresh oregano

Salt and pepper to taste

1 pound fusilli pasta

7 ounces freshly grated mozzarella cheese

½ cup freshly grated Parmesan cheese

1. In a large skillet over medium heat, heat the oil and simmer the tomatoes, oregano, and salt and pepper for about 20 minutes, stirring occasionally. Remove the skillet from heat and set aside.

2. In a large pot of boiling water, cook the pasta until al denté, 6 to 8 minutes. Drain the pasta.

3. Add the pasta to the tomato mixture and return it to the stove. Over medium heat, cook the pasta and tomatoes for 3 minutes, stirring frequently. Remove the pasta from heat and add the mozzarella and Parmesan, tossing well to combine.

PASTA WITH FRESH RICOTTA CHEESE
Penne e Ricotta   SERVES 4

1 pound penne pasta

1 cup whole milk

12 ounces fresh ricotta cheese

1 tablespoon sugar

1 teaspoon ground cinnamon

Salt and pepper to taste

1 tablespoon chopped fresh
  marjoram

1. Cook the penne in a large pot of boiling water until al denté, 6 to 8 minutes. Drain the pasta.

2. While the pasta is cooking, in a medium mixing bowl, combine the milk, ricotta, sugar, cinnamon, salt and pepper, and marjoram. Using a rubber spatula, mix the ingredients well.

3. Add the cooked pasta to the ricotta mixture and toss to combine, then return the mixture to the pot over low heat for 2 minutes.

RIGATONI IN SPICY CAULIFLOWER SAUCE
Rigatoni al Cavolfiore

SERVES 4

1 medium cauliflower

1 medium onion, chopped

2 tablespoons olive oil

2 tablespoons butter

3 garlic cloves, crushed

½ teaspoon crushed red pepper

Salt and pepper to taste

1 pound fresh rigatoni pasta

1. Divide the cauliflower into florets and stalks, and chop the stalks roughly.
2. Cook the florets and stalks in boiling water for 8 minutes, then drain and set aside.
3. In a large skillet over medium heat, sauté the onion in oil and butter until soft. Add the garlic and red pepper, and sauté until the garlic is lightly browned.
4. Add the cooked cauliflower and cook for an additional 10 minutes. Season with salt and pepper.
5. While the cauliflower is cooking in step 4, add the pasta to a large pot of boiling water and cook for 6 to 8 minutes, or until al denté.
7. Drain the pasta and add to the cauliflower in the saucepan. Reduce the heat to medium-low, and cook for an additional 2 minutes while tossing constantly. Transfer the pasta to a large serving platter and serve while hot.

SPAGHETTI WITH GARLIC AND OIL
Spaghetti con Aglio Olio

SERVES 4 AS A MAIN COURSE
OR 6 AS AN APPETIZER

1 pound spaghetti
½ cup olive oil
4 garlic cloves, chopped
Pinch of crushed red pepper

Salt and black pepper to taste
½ cup chopped fresh parsley
Grated Parmesan cheese to taste

1. In a medium pasta pot, boil water and add the spaghetti. Cook until al denté, 6 to 8 minutes. Drain the pasta.
2. Heat the oil in a large skillet over medium heat. Add the garlic and sauté for 2 minutes. Be careful not to overcook the garlic or the taste will be dramatically altered.
3. Reduce the heat under the garlic mixture to low, and add the red pepper and salt and black pepper. Simmer for 2 to 3 minutes.
4. Add the pasta to the skillet, still over low heat. Toss the pasta with parsley, add a pinch of Parmesan cheese, and serve hot.

BAKED PASTA WITH EGGPLANT
Timballo di Pasta e Melanzane
SERVES 6

1 pound eggplant

2 tablespoons sea salt

1 pound ripe tomatoes

2 cups olive oil

Salt to taste

1 pound rigatoni pasta

4 garlic cloves

10 fresh basil leaves, finely
 chopped

Pepper to taste

1 cup dry bread crumbs

1 cup grated pecorino cheese

1. Preheat the oven to 375°F.

2. Slice the eggplant into ½-inch slices and place the slices on a cutting board. Sprinkle with sea salt and set aside.

3. Drop the tomatoes into a large pot of boiling water for 1 minute, then rinse them under cold running water. This will help loosen the tomato skins for easier peeling. Peel the tomatoes and cut in halves width-wise, squeezing out as many seeds as possible, then cut again into eighths.

4. In a medium frying pan, heat ¼ cup of the olive oil and fry the egg-plant slices until brown, adding oil as necessary, but reserving ¼ cup. Drain the slices on a double layer of paper towels.

5. In a large pot, boil water and add salt and the pasta. Cook for 4 min-utes. (It won't be done—will finish cooking in juice while baking.) Drain the pasta and set aside.

6. Over medium heat in a medium saucepan, sauté the garlic in the re-maining ¼ cup olive oil until browned, then add the tomatoes and basil. Season with salt and pepper, and cook over medium heat for 10 minutes.

7. Butter a lasagna pan. Spoon tomato sauce generously into the pan so that the bottom is thinly covered. Combine the pasta with the remaining tomatoes, and put a layer of pasta on the bottom of the pan, then cover with a layer of eggplant slices.

8. Repeat this process until the eggplant and pasta are completely used, ending with a layer of eggplant on top.

9. Sprinkle with the bread crumbs and cheese.

10. Bake the casserole for 25 minutes, and serve hot or warm.

OVEN-COOKED SPINACH FETTUCCINE WITH HAM, CREAM, AND EGGS
Pasticcio di Fettuccine Verde al Prosciutto

SERVES 4

4 eggs, separated

8 ounces ham, cubed

2 tablespoon chopped fresh parsley

Pinch of nutmeg (optional)

Salt and pepper to taste

1 cup heavy cream

1 pound spinach fettuccini

¼ cup butter

Parmesan cheese to taste

1. Preheat the oven to 350°F.
2. Combine the beaten egg yolks, ham, and parsley in a medium saucepan over medium heat, and stir with a wooden spoon, cooking for 3 to 4 minutes. Add the nutmeg and salt and pepper. Remove from the heat.
3. In a medium mixing bowl, whip the cream until it forms stiff peaks. In a separate bowl, whip the egg whites until stiff. Carefully stir the whipped cream into the egg whites and fold into the ham mixture.
4. Cook the pasta in a large pot of salted, boiling water for 6 to 8 minutes. Drain.
5. Grease a casserole pan with butter and spread the pasta on the bottom.
6. Cover the pasta with the ham mixture and sprinkle with Parmesan cheese.
7. Bake for 45 minutes, and serve hot.

5

FOWL
UNDER THE TUSCAN SUN

My sons and I recently made our first pilgrimage to Italy, the country of our heritage. The trip was an eye-opener in that it taught me much about my ancestors' origins. Mom's side came from Casina, while Dad's family originated from Naples and Rome.

I'd never dreamed of going to Italy until the moment I saw Under the Tuscan Sun. I'd wanted to see for myself if that region was as beautiful as it was portrayed. So, when we began to plan our trip, I insisted that we include Tuscany in our itinerary.

The central region of Italy embodies beauty and history; rolling hills with olive groves and vineyards as far as you can see. It wasn't at all surprising to learn that this land produces some of the best wines and olive oil in the world. Tuscany resembles one great big walled hill situated in the middle of nowhere, with its carefully tended fields dotted with picturesque rural hamlets and walled medieval towns.

In Tuscany, I was introduced to Italian country cooking. I quickly learned that natives of the region value their rich cuisine as much as their incredible art and architecture and the dazzling countryside. Such edible art is a delight to all the senses—beautiful to behold, fragrant with fresh herbs and spices, and tantalizing to even the most fast food–dulled taste buds.

Tuscans are epicures, and glorious, delicious meals are a big part of their daily life. Their idea of home cooking is peasant dishes like Ribollita (page 134) and Panzanella (page 13), served family style. Most traditional dishes include such common ingredients as different kinds of beans, homegrown vegetables, fresh herbs, fruity olive oil, roasted meats, and fresh, crusty breads. This simple peasant fare—possibly one of Italy's best-kept secrets—comes from generations of family recipes, all cooked and served with love.

While Tuscan cuisine may not be as exotic as truffles and caviar, it is a masterful blend of presentation and incredible taste. This section includes my favorite Tuscan fowl dish, Fagiano alle Olive Nere *(page 79), a succulent pheasant dish with black olives and crushed tomatoes, along with some of the other Italian chicken and fowl dishes that I love.

CHICKEN WITH MUSHROOMS, PEPPERS, AND WINE

Pollo alla Cacciatora

SERVES 6

2 large chickens, cut in eighths

½ cup vegetable oil

2 cups sliced white mushrooms

2 green bell peppers, seeds removed, sliced into 1-inch strips

2 red bell peppers, seeds removed, sliced into 1-inch strips

1 large onion, chopped

1 cup white wine

2 chicken bouillon cubes

2 cups hot water

One 28-ounce can crushed tomatoes, undrained

½ teaspoon dried oregano

Pinch of red pepper

2 tablespoons chopped fresh Italian parsley

Salt and pepper to taste

1. Wash the chicken pieces and pat dry with paper towels.
2. In a large skillet, heat the oil over medium-high heat. Add the chicken and cook in batches of 3 to 4 pieces, turning often, for about 12 minutes per batch.
3. Add the mushrooms, peppers, and onion, and sauté for 5 minutes, stirring to avoid sticking.
4. Add the white wine and sauté for another 2 minutes.
5. Dissolve the chicken bouillon in the hot water, and add it to the skillet. Add the tomatoes, oregano, red pepper, parsley flakes, and salt and pepper, and bring to a boil.
6. Reduce the heat to low, and simmer, uncovered, for 30 minutes. Serve hot.

CHICKEN WITH SAUSAGE AND PEPPERS
Pollo alla Scarpariello   SERVES 6

1½ cups vegetable oil

1 pound sweet Italian sausage links

1 large onion, chopped

2 medium chickens, cut in eighths

2 red bell peppers, seeds removed, sliced into 1-inch strips

2 yellow bell peppers, seeds removed, sliced into 1-inch strips

1 chicken bouillon cube

½ cup hot water

2 garlic cloves, minced

½ cup white wine

½ teaspoon chopped fresh oregano

½ cup white vinegar

Salt and pepper to taste

1. In a large skillet, heat the oil, sausage, and onion over medium-high heat for 8 minutes. Remove the sausage from the pan and set aside to drain.

2. Add the chicken to the onion mixture and fry for 15 minutes, stirring occasionally.

3. Add the red and yellow peppers and sauté for an additional 5 minutes.

4. Drain the excess oil from skillet. Dissolve the chicken bouillion in the hot water, and add it to the skillet, along with the sausage, garlic, and wine. Bring to a boil.

5. Add the oregano, vinegar, and salt and pepper. Reduce the heat to medium-low, and allow the mixture in the skillet to simmer for 12 minutes.

6. Transfer the chicken scarpariello to a large platter and serve hot.

PHEASANT WITH BLACK OLIVES
Fagiano alle Olive Nere   SERVES 4

One 2-pound pheasant
Salt and pepper to taste
¼ cup flour
¼ cup olive oil
1 large white onion, diced
⅔ cup white wine

One 28-ounce can crushed tomatoes, undrained
1 beef bouillon cube
1 cup hot water
4 ounces black olives, whole and pitted

1. Clean the pheasant and season with salt and pepper, then sprinkle with flour.
2. In a large skillet over medium heat, heat the olive oil and sauté the onion for 3 minutes or until the onion is soft. Add the pheasant and sauté on both sides for an additional 5 minutes.
3. Add the wine and cook until the wine is absorbed. Stir in the tomatoes and season with salt.
4. Partially cover the skillet and cook over medium heat for 45 minutes.
5. During the last 15 minutes of step 4, dissolve the bouillon in the hot water to make beef stock. Slowly add the stock as the sauce thickens.
6. Add the olives and stir well, and cook for an additional 15 minutes.
7. Remove the pheasant from the skillet and cut into quarters. Return the pieces to the sauce and reheat over medium heat. Serve hot, with a rice side and a leafy green salad.

STUFFED ROASTED LEMON CHICKEN

Pollo Arrosto al Limone   SERVES 8

2 large fresh whole chickens

½ teaspoon salt, plus more to
taste

½ cup lemon juice

1½ teaspoons black pepper, plus
more to taste

1 teaspoon chopped fresh parsley

1 stick unsalted butter

½ cup chopped celery

1 carrot, chopped

½ cup chicken broth

1 teaspoon dried oregano

6 slices white bread, broken into
crouton-size pieces

1. Preheat the oven to 350°F.

2. Scrub the chickens in cold water. In a large soup pot, add the chickens, enough water to cover the meat, and ½ teaspoon of the salt. Bring to a boil and cook until the chickens are tender, or about 12 minutes.

3. In a small mixing bowl, combine the lemon juice, ½ teaspoon of the black pepper, salt to taste, and the parsley, and whisk well. Set aside.

4. Remove the chickens and place in a large roasting pan. Baste the chicken with the lemon juice mixture, making sure to spread parsley and pepper on all sides of the chickens including the bottom, and bake for 30 minutes.

5. In a medium skillet, melt the butter over low heat and sauté the celery, carrot, and chicken broth. Add the oregano and 1 teaspoon of the black pepper, and cook over medium heat for 4 minutes, or until celery and carrots are tender. Remove from heat.

6. In a medium mixing bowl, combine the carrot mixture and white bread, kneading well with hands.

7. Remove the chickens from the oven and let cool for 20 minutes. Baste the chickens with the lemon-pepper mixture again. Using a wooden

spoon, spoon the bread mixture into the chicken. Replace chickens in the oven, and bake for an additional 30 minutes.

8. Baste the chickens again immediately before serving. Serve cut into quarters, spooning stuffing onto each plate.

CHICKEN STUFFED WITH HAM AND CHEESE
Pollo Rollatini

2½ pounds chicken cutlets, pounded thin

½ pound sliced mozzarella

½ pound prosciutto, sliced

¼ cup chopped fresh parsley

Salt and pepper to taste

2 eggs, beaten

2 cups dry bread crumbs

¼ cup olive oil

1. Lay the chicken cutlets flat, and stack each with 1 slice of mozzarella and 1 slice of prosciutto. Garnish each stack with a pinch of parsley and salt and pepper, and roll the stacks up, with the chicken cutlet on the outside. Secure the stacks with a toothpick through the center.

2. Put the eggs in a small bowl and season with salt and pepper. Place the bread crumbs in another small bowl. Dip each rolled chicken cutlet first in the egg batter and then in bread crumbs. Repeat this step so that each cutlet is dipped twice in the egg and bread crumbs.

3. Heat the olive oil in large skillet over medium heat.

4. Using tongs, carefully place the rolled chicken cutlets in the hot oil, cover the skillet, and cook for 4 to 5 minutes on each side or until golden. Remove the fried cutlets with a slotted spoon, and place on a double layer of paper towels to drain any excess oil before serving.

6

RISOTTO

MY ROMAN HOLIDAY

No one told me Leonardo daVinci Airport was one of Rome's hot spots, but I found out for myself as soon as I walked into the terminal. The place is barely *air-conditioned. Neither was the bus that transported my boys and me—and our* Growing Up Gotti *film crew—to our five-star hotel. The hotel wasn't air-conditioned either—at least not the way I expected a luxury hostelry to be in 90-degree heat. Our second night there, I had to prevail upon the goodwill of the concierge—who happened to be the only person on duty in the whole grand hotel—to bring an ordinary oscillating fan to my room at 4 A.M. so I could finally get some sleep. And, though our genial drivers assured us the A/C was on full blast, the cabs we took to see the sights and visit the chic shops on the Via Veneto were sweltering!*

I'm not saying my Roman holiday wasn't wonderful—it's one of the most cosmopolitan, beautiful cities I've ever seen, with something wonderful to see around every corner—but this New York gal, who, I admit, is used to her creature comforts, was puzzled that the Romans hardly seemed to notice the heat. Even the stores and restaurants that advertised air-conditioning were barely cool!

It wasn't until we were packing to leave the Eternal City for the next stop on our Tour d'Italia that I learned why the supercooled air we Americans take for granted is virtually nonexistent. By American standards, there's a power shortage. The power plants can't generate enough electricity to air-condition every hotel, shop, restaurant, airport, and home. If they could, the cost of fuel to run the plants would be prohibi-

tive, which is also why most automotive air-conditioning is barely there. Let's just say I'll never complain about my outrageous electric bill again. In comparison to my stay in Rome, the Long Island Power Authority offers a cool deal.

It's easy to see why Rome has been labeled the Eternal City. The physical beauty of this ageless city abounds. There is so much history to see: the Coliseum, Pantheon, Sistine Chapel, and Vatican, not to mention the Piazza di Spagna (the beautiful Spanish Steps). It's easy to see why tourists toss coins into the exquisite Trevi Fountain to bring them love and guarantee their return to Rome, time and again.

One of the oldest cities in the world, Rome is a top vacation destination for Americans—especially Italian-Americans, as I could see. I noticed them strolling the piazzas to sip rich espressos and sample delectable Roman cuisine while exploring the many architectural treasures and works of art that fill the city.

Rome is an exquisite fusion of the history of civilization in every imaginable form: cultural, religious, military, governmental, and economical. On one hand, it's the bustling cosmopolitan seat of Italian government and trade, and on the other it's as traditionally old-world Italian as I imagined.

Rome is hardly laid-back or slow paced. It's bustling with as much energy as I've felt in other fast-paced, highly cosmopolitan cities such as New York, Miami, and Chicago. The exception is from noon to three every afternoon: that's when Romans leave work, shopkeepers close their stores, and everyone takes a leisurely stroll homeward for a beautifully prepared meal or to a piazza for a picnic of fresh bread and fruit with cheese and, yes, a bit of rich red vino.

Considering how much work is conducted over lunch in the United States—and how often we grab a pack of crackers and a cup of coffee from the vending machine and work through lunchtime at our desks—this dedication to a three-hour midday siesta seems peculiar.

Romans take their food and drink as seriously as any culture world-

wide. This lunchtime break has become the talk of many fast-paced cultures for the way the city shuts down for the sake of great food, aged booze, and R&R. Yet while I was there, I could understand why when in Rome, it's good to do as the Romans do. You see, as much as there is to see and do in the daytime, there's a wonderful *life that goes on into the night.*

If you want a break from the metropolitan pace of the city proper, you don't have to drive longer than ten minutes beyond the city limits and you'll find yourself inhaling the fragrant country air, lost in the vision of grassy fields of sunflowers, brilliant under the blazing sun, and the limitless green fields of wheat. This too is Rome, and it forces tourists to return again and again and locals to never want to leave.

Roman cooking is quite different from the Tuscan and Florentine methods in that Roman cuisine is contemporary in both look and taste. Such classics as crusty Roman bread or Romano cheese–flavored pasta dishes will never become obsolete. However, because of Romans' strong desire to keep up with the changing face and taste of contemporary cuisine, you may find the food in Rome is modernized, while still rooted in tradition.

Roman food does not rely on thick, rich sauces to overpower the basic flavors of foods. The sauces, like basic pomodoro (tomato sauce), are simple, fresh, and meant only to complement whatever dish they accompany. Romans are less traditional when it comes to preparing and cooking their foods as well. They are constantly changing the taste of their recipes by experimenting with different ingredients in different dishes. For example, by using Pecorino Romano instead of Parmesan or using fresh tomatoes instead of canned, chicken instead of veal, Roman cooks offer a wonderful variety on their tables. Italy's self-described modernists, Romans believe no recipe is etched in stone, nor should family-style dining be the rule. They are not afraid to try something new or break with tradition.

Perhaps that's the reason Roman food is one of my favorites in all of

Italy. I can honestly say no two Roman recipes have tasted the same, even when prepared by the same chef! This chapter includes some of my favorite Roman risotto recipes—like Risotto con le Pere *(page 87) and* Risotto con le Zucchine *(page 88), as well as many other classic risotto dishes.*

RISOTTO WITH PEARS

Risotto con le Pere   SERVES 4 AS A MAIN DISH OR 6 AS A SIDE DISH

2 tablespoon butter

1 medium onion, chopped

2 cups Arborio rice

1 cup dry white wine

6 cups vegetable stock, kept at a
   simmer

4 medium pears, peeled, cored,
   and cubed

2 teaspoons pear juice

Salt and pepper to taste

3 ounces fontina cheese

¼ cup pear liqueur

1. In a large skillet over medium heat, melt the butter and sauté the onion. Stir in the rice and sauté for 4 minutes.

2. Add the wine and bring the simmering vegetable stock to a boil. When the wine has been all absorbed, add ½ cup of the boiling stock and the pears and pear juice. Allow the risotto to simmer, uncovered, for 10 minutes, stirring occasionally.

3. As the liquid in the skillet evaporates, add the remainder of the vegetable stock ½ cup at a time, and continue cooking for an additional 15 minutes, stirring occasionally.

4. Season with salt and pepper, and add the fontina cheese and liqueur. Stir well and serve hot.

ZUCCHINI RISOTTO

Risotto con le Zucchine   SERVES 4 AS A MAIN DISH OR 6 AS A SIDE DISH

2 tablespoons olive oil

2 ounces pancetta, diced

1 garlic clove, chopped

1 medium onion, chopped

1 pound zucchini, diced

2 cups Arborio rice

1 cup white wine

6 cups vegetable stock, kept at a simmer

Salt and pepper to taste

½ cup grated Parmesan cheese

Fresh chopped parsley to taste

1. In a large skillet over medium heat, heat the oil and sauté the pancetta for 4 minutes.

2. Add the garlic, onion, and zucchini and sauté for an additional 7 minutes, stirring occasionally so that the ingredients do not stick and burn.

3. Stir in the rice and sauté for 3 minutes, stirring constantly, then add the wine and continue to cook. When the wine is nearly all absorbed, stir in ½ cup of the hot vegetable stock and cook, uncovered, stirring occasionally, for 10 minutes.

4. When the stock is nearly absorbed, add another ½ cup of the vegetable stock and simmer, uncovered, for an additional 15 minutes. As the stock evaporates while cooking, add additional stock by the ½ cup, stirring occasionally, until the risotto is cooked and has reached the desired creamy consistency.

5. Add salt and pepper, sprinkle with Parmesan cheese and parsley, and serve immediately.

RISOTTO WITH FRESH ASPARAGUS

Risotto con Asparagi SERVES 6 AS AN APPETIZER OR 4 AS A MAIN COURSE

¾ *pound fresh asparagus, cleaned and ends trimmed*

2 *tablespoons unsalted butter*

2 *tablespoons extra-virgin olive oil*

3 *tablespoons finely minced onion*

2 *cups Arborio rice*

4 *chicken bouillon cubes*

½ *cup freshly grated Parmesan cheese*

Black pepper to taste

Salt to taste

1. Place the asparagus in a medium saucepan, and add cold water until the asparagus is covered by 1 inch of water. Bring the water to a boil over medium-high heat. Once the water is boiling, cover the pan, reduce the heat, and let it simmer for about 5 minutes, or until the asparagus is tender but still firm.

2. Gently remove the asparagus and let it cool, reserving the cooking water in the pan.

3. Cut the cooled asparagus into 1-inch pieces and set aside.

4. Add enough fresh water to the asparagus cooking water to make 6 cups. Place this in a medium saucepan over low heat to keep warm.

5. Heat the butter and oil in another medium saucepan over medium heat. Add the onion, and sauté for about 3½ minutes, or until the onion is translucent.

6. Add the rice to the saucepan with the onion and sauté for about 3 minutes, stirring constantly.

7. Dissolve the chicken bouillon cubes in 1½ cups of the asparagus cooking water, and add to the rice. Continue stirring the rice, allowing the liquid to evaporate.

8. Continue cooking the risotto, adding ½ cup of the hot asparagus cooking water at a time as the liquid evaporates. Continue this process, stirring constantly, until the rice is the desired creamy consistency. This can take 20 to 30 minutes.

9. Remove the risotto from the heat, and stir in the asparagus pieces.

10. Blend in the Parmesan cheese, black pepper, and, if necessary, a pinch of salt as needed. Serve immediately.

These days risotto (a combination of rice and pasta) dishes stand on their own as the main course or entrée. For most people, however, risotto is a very filling dish and therefore is consumed in smaller portions, as a side or appetizer. I, for one, most enjoy a meal when there are multiple choices to sample. For those who enjoy this dish alone, a light salad as an accompaniment produces a hearty, full meal—especially on cold nights!

TOMATO RISOTTO
Risotto al Pomodoro

SERVES 4 AS A MAIN DISH OR 6 AS A SIDE DISH

⅓ cup butter

2 tablespoons olive oil

1 medium onion, chopped

2 garlic cloves, minced

6 fresh basil leaves

2 cups Arborio rice

5 beef bouillon cubes

5 cups hot water

1 pound ripe plum tomatoes,
  peeled and chopped

Salt and pepper to taste

¼ cup grated Parmesan cheese

1. Melt 2½ tablespoons of the butter in a medium skillet, and add the oil, onion, garlic, and basil. Sauté over medium heat for 5 minutes.

2. Add the rice and cook for 2 minutes, stirring occasionally. Dissolve the bouillon cubes in the hot water, and stir the resulting beef broth into the rice, along with the tomatoes. Cook uncovered, stirring occasionally, for 15 to 20 minutes, or until the rice is tender.

3. When the rice is cooked, stir in the remaining 2½ tablespoons butter, salt and pepper, and cheese, and serve.

VEGETABLE RISOTTO

SERVES 6

4 cups water

4 cups Arborio rice

¼ cup olive oil

1 white onion, chopped

1 celery stalk, chopped

1 cup chopped carrots

¼ pound bacon, cut into small
pieces

2 tablespoon chopped fresh
parsley

Salt and pepper to taste

1 pound ripe plum tomatoes,
peeled and chopped

1 cup fresh peas

1. In a medium saucepan, bring the water to a boil. Add the Arborio rice, cover the pan, and simmer for 2 to 3 minutes, or until water is absorbed and rice feels soft and fluffy. Set the pan aside, still covered.

2. In a large skillet, heat the olive oil over medium heat. Sauté the onion, celery, carrots, bacon, and parsley for 3–5 minutes.

3. Add the tomatoes to the skillet, and cook for an additional 25 minutes, covered.

4. Add the peas and salt and pepper to taste, and cook for an additional 15 minutes.

5. Add the rice and stir to combine all the ingredients. Continue cooking over low heat for 2 minutes, stirring frequently.

7

SEAFOOD

THE DAILY CATCH

One of the most memorable stops we made in Italy was Positano/ Capri. The drive up the coast from Naples included some of the most magnificent sightseeing I've ever viewed. It felt like scenes in the movies when Grace Kelly takes a drive with Cary Grant, convertible zipping along the cliffside, kerchief tied around her head—romance, romance, romance abounds! The colorful cliffside villas and delightful sunsets by the sea are magnificent! But one of the most delectable treats for the locals and tourists is sampling the "fresh from the water" fish, deliciously prepared—right by the water's edge. I'm not kidding! Pull up a rowboat after a day at Capri and devour freshly caught, cleaned, and grilled calamari. It melts in your mouth! Positano is known for this delightful tourist trap and all its pebble-lined beaches.

Fish is a great Italian dish—its light, healthful, and calorie-pleasing for those watching their bulging waistlines. Some of Italy's best sauces are used with fish dishes, and some of Italy's best dishes are made with fish. While Italy is not always equated with seaside towns, the fresh seafood there produces the most mouthwatering recipes ever!

LINGUINE WITH WHITE CLAM SAUCE
Linguine Vongole

SERVES 6

2½ dozen littleneck clams
1 cup virgin olive oil
1 garlic clove, crushed
One 8-ounce bottle clam juice
¼ cup dry white wine
1 pound fresh linguine

Two 6.5-ounce cans of chopped clams
½ teaspoon dried oregano
12 fresh parsley leaves, chopped
Salt and pepper to taste

1. Wash the unopened clams and set them in a pot filled with cold water for 30 minutes to soak off any excess dirt. Discard any that are already open or have cracked shells.
2. Put the washed clams in a large pot with ½ cup water. Cover and bring to a boil. Simmer over medium heat until the clams open. Discard any unopened clams.
3. In a large saucepan over medium heat, heat the olive oil and sauté the garlic. Add the clam juice and the white wine, and keep warm over medium heat.
4. Boil water and add the linguine, cooking for 6 to 8 minutes, or until the pasta is al denté. Drain the pasta.
5. While the pasta is cooking, add the opened clams, canned clams and their juices, oregano, and parsley to the sautéed garlic. Stir and simmer for about 6 minutes, until the sauce is well combined and heated through.
6. Add the drained pasta to the clam saucepan and reduce the heat to low, quickly tossing the pasta. Add salt and pepper. As with most pasta sauces, be sure to add the pasta to the sauce (not the other way around) and continue cooking for 1 minute or so—this last step will guarantee maximum flavor!

PENNE WITH SEAFOOD AND VEGETABLES
Penne con Pesce e Verdure   SERVES 4

1 dozen littleneck clams

⅓ cup olive oil

1 medium onion, diced

1 large red bell pepper, seeded
  and diced

1 large zucchini, cut into ½-inch
  pieces

12 ounces squid, cleaned and
  sliced into 1½-inch pieces

Salt and pepper to taste

½ cup white wine

8 ounces jumbo shrimp, cleaned
  and deveined

2 tablespoons chopped fresh
  parsley

1 pound penne pasta

1. Wash the unopened clams and set them in pot filled with cold water
   for 30 minutes to soak off any excess dirt. Discard any that are already
   open or have cracked shells.

2. In a large skillet, heat the olive oil and sauté the onion until it turns
   translucent. Add the bell pepper and zucchini and cook for an additional 6 minutes, stirring to avoid burning.

3. Add the squid and unopened clams to the skillet. Season with salt and
   pepper, and cook for an additional 5 minutes.

4. Add the wine and cover the skillet, cooking for an additional 10 minutes.

5. Add the shrimp and parsley. Cook for an additional 5 minutes, until
   the shrimp are cooked and appear opaque and rosy.

6. Cook the pasta in a large pot of boiling water according to package
   directions, until al denté, 6–8 minutes. Drain the pasta and set it
   aside.

7. Using a slotted spoon, remove the clams (which should now be open; discard any closed clams) from the mixture. Discard the shells and return the cooked clams to the mixture.

8. Add the cooked penne to the skillet, and toss well to distribute the seafood among the pasta. Cook over low heat for an additional 5 minutes.

SEAFOOD SALAD
Frutti di Mare

SERVES 4 TO 6 AS A SIDE DISH

1 pound fresh calamari, cleaned and tentacles discarded

2 cups lemon juice

2 teaspoons salt, plus more to taste

10 jumbo shrimp, cleaned and deveined

1 cup olive oil

2 garlic cloves, minced

1½ teaspoons chopped fresh parsley

Pepper to taste

1 cup crabmeat

One 1½-pound lobster, cooked and meat removed from shell

1 lemon, cut into 6 wedges

1. Fill a medium saucepan with water and add the calamari, ¼ cup of the lemon juice, and 2 teaspoons of the salt. Bring the liquid to a boil, then reduce the heat to medium-low and continue cooking for 5 additional minutes.

2. Remove the pot from the heat, and rinse the calamari with cold water. Drain and cut the calamari into small rings. Refrigerate the rings for 20 minutes.

3. In another medium saucepan, boil water and cook the shrimp for 2 minutes, then drain and cut each shrimp into 4 pieces.

4. In a medium mixing bowl, add the calamari, shrimp, oil, remaining 1¾ cups lemon juice, garlic, parsley, and salt and pepper, and toss to coat the seafood.

5. Remove the calamari and shrimp with a slotted spoon, and set aside in a separate bowl.

6. Add the crabmeat and lobster meat to the oil mixture, and toss to coat.

7. Return the calamari and shrimp back to the bowl with the crabmeat and lobster, and toss to combine all. Serve with lemon wedges for garnish.

FUSILLI WITH JUMBO SHRIMP
Fusilli al Gambero Rosso

SERVES 4

1 pound fresh fusilli pasta
¼ cup olive oil
¼ cup chopped fresh parsley
4 garlic cloves

1 pound jumbo shrimp, peeled and deveined
Salt and pepper to taste
2 tablespoons butter

1. Cook the pasta in a pot of boiling water until it is al denté, 6 to 8 minutes. Drain the pasta.

2. While the pasta is cooking, heat the oil in a medium skillet over low heat. Sauté the parsley and garlic in the oil for 3 minutes, stirring often to avoid burning the ingredients.

3. Chop one quarter of the shrimp. Add all the shrimp (chopped and whole) to the pan along with salt and pepper, and cook, covered, for 5 minutes.

4. Add the pasta to the skillet and stir to combine the ingredients, then cook for an additional 2 to 3 minutes. Add the butter and toss the ingredients to combine. Transfer the pasta and juices to a serving platter, and serve hot.

PAPPARDELLE WITH TUNA SAUCE
Pappardelle Tonnato

½ cup olive oil

½ cup capers, drained

One 6-ounce can tuna in oil

1 pound fresh pappardelle pasta

1 lemon

2 anchovies

1. In a medium skillet, heat the olive oil and sauté the capers and tuna for 2 minutes, stirring constantly.

2. In a medium pasta pot, boil water and cook the pasta until al denté, 6 to 8 minutes.

3. Drain and add the cooked pasta to the tuna mixture in the skillet.

4. Slice the lemon in half and squeeze the juice of one half into the skillet. Thinly slice the other half.

5. Transfer the pasta to a platter, garnishing with thin lemon slices and anchovies.

PASTA WITH SARDINES
Pasta con le Sarde

SERVES 4 TO 6

4 anchovies

½ pound sardines

½ cup olive oil

1 white onion, chopped

½ cup raisins

½ cup pine nuts

Pinch of salt

Handful of fennel leaves

Pinch of powdered saffron

1 teaspoon crushed red pepper

1 pound fresh fusilli pasta

1 garlic clove, chopped

Handful of dry bread crumbs

1. Preheat the oven to 350°F.
2. Fillet the anchovies and sardines, removing the heads and tails.
3. In a large skillet, heat 4 tablespoons of the oil and sauté the onion. Add the sardines anchovies, garlic, raisins, pine nuts, salt, most of the fennel leaves, saffron, and red pepper. Cover and let simmer for 12 minutes.
4. In a large pot, boil the water and cook the pasta until al denté, 6 to 8 minutes. Add a few fennel leaves to flavor the pasta water.
5. Drain the pasta and transfer to a baking platter or casserole dish. Mix with the anchovy and sardine mixture. Sprinkle the pasta with bread crumbs and bake for an additional 10 minutes.

CODFISH STEW
Baccalá

3½ pounds baccalá (dried salt cod)

8 large baking potatoes, peeled and cut in eighths

1 cup olive oil

1 bunch fresh celery, ends trimmed and stalks cut into 2-inch pieces

1 large onion, chopped

2 cups Greek black olives, pitted and cut in halves

Four 28-ounce cans crushed tomatoes, undrained

10 chicken bouillon cubes

10 cups hot water

Salt to taste

1. Cut the *baccalá* into 2- to 3-inch pieces and soak in 2 quarts of cold water for 24 hours. Drain and rinse.

2. Place the cut potatoes in water and boil for about 15 minutes or until the potatoes are soft.

3. In a large saucepan, heat the oil over medium heat. Add the celery, and sauté for 5 minutes.

4. Add the onion and olives, and sauté for 1 to 2 minutes. Stir in the tomatoes and bring to a boil.

5. Dissolve the bouillion cubes in 2 cups of the hot water, and add it to the tomato sauce with the remaining 8 cups hot water, boiled potatoes, and *baccalá*. Stir the ingredients to combine, and allow to simmer for 10 minutes.

6. Season with salt if desired. Serve with a risotto or green vegetable side dish.

Leave plenty of time for this stew. The codfish needs to soak for a whole day to cut its saltiness.

8

MEATS

A LADY IN THE KITCHEN, A WHORE IN THE BEDROOM

*I'm often asked a lot of questions about my father: What was he like?
What made him tick? Rarely am I asked about my mother, so I often re-
fer to her as "my unsung hero." When I was a young girl growing up, my
mother taught me some very valuable lessons—mostly about how good
girls should behave. It was a constant stream of "Good girls don't do
this" and "Good girls don't do that." Well, I'm sorry to say I spent so
much time worrying about being a "good girl," I missed out on much fun
in my lifetime. I was one of those girls who saved herself for marriage.*

*My mother's voice kept playing in my mind and the enormous guilt
was enough to scare the bejesus out of me! All kidding aside, not all the
lessons I learned from Mom had to do with sex (and staying a "good
Catholic schoolgirl"). I learned to cook when I was eight years old. Mom
felt I was ready (well, thinking back, maybe she didn't—I remember
nagging her every night at dinnertime to let me help her cook. Perhaps
she just grew tired of hearing me whine).*

*In retrospect, it was one of the most valuable lessons Mom taught me.
Being an "old-fashioned" woman herself, Mom used many an opportu-
nity, each time we were in the kitchen, to instill in me the importance of
being self-sufficient and able to take care of your own family. Mom truly
believed if a woman didn't know how to cook by the time the official honeymoon was over, there was sure to be a divorce decree stuffed in a large
manila envelope waiting for her in the mailbox the moment she returned.*

It's not unusual in Italy to teach your daughters to cook at age seven. With some marriages being prearranged by the time a girl is thirteen, this expertise given to you by your mother was considered a luxury—a wealth of invaluable information. A good cook is considered a "great catch" as far as being a wife goes. My mother taught me almost everything I know about cooking—including the sermons about how important it is to cook for your family with "love in your heart." She let me know early on that the most important thing a woman can do for her family is nurture, shelter, and care for her loved ones unconditionally. She constantly reminded me that it wasn't "beneath a wife to prepare and put a hot meal on the table for her husband the moment he walked through the door" at six or seven, after a hard day's work. Mom believed it was the least a woman could do for her man considering he was out in the cold (or heat) all day, breaking his ass, trying to make enough to pay the bills and put money on the table at the end of the week. She considered it a wife's duty to buy fresh ingredients to put a delicious and hearty meal on the table night after night. After all, she reasoned, "it was his money that paid for the food."

Whenever my dad would head home at night, he would give Mom a "heads up" by calling her on the phone and letting her know he was minutes away by car. This was her signal to set the table and transfer the fresh soups, sauces, and cuts of meat to the table. My mother loved my father so much that this simple routine, believe it or not, brought her much joy. She loved seeing the look on Dad's face when he sat at the table and eyed some of his favorite dishes. Next, he'd listen intently so he could hear the sound of running water coming from his upstairs bathroom. Coming home to a hearty meal and a hot bath were luxuries Dad never took for granted. He was the first to brag to anyone who'd listen about "what a lucky man he was to be married to such a caring and thoughtful wife."

My mother's beliefs were not understood and accepted by everyone. My sister Angel was a bit more "liberated" than Mom and I. She thought waiting on a man hand and foot was "degrading and demeaning." Angel was of the belief that men and women "were created equal" and she felt men should toe their end of the line at home just like a woman. She believed that in a society where most housewives and moms were forced to take on full- and part-time jobs so they could hold their own with respect to the household expenses, the men should do their part, too. Because of the diversity in opinion, the house could become quite boisterous with the three of us arguing. But, no matter what, my sister wouldn't cave and kept her mindset fixated on the whole women's lib thing. She let my mother know that when the day came that she got married, her husband would have to accept the fact she was a "liberated woman"—and if he wanted a hearty meal and a hot running bath, "he would have to do both for himself."

Mom tried to reason with Angel over the years—especially just before her wedding to her first husband. Mom felt the young women of today could and should take a lesson from the women of yesterday (namely, their moms). Mom gave her the "marriage is an equal partnership" speech (fifty-fifty; a man provides, while a woman keeps house) so often that I could recite the stats if quizzed! She explained that when it comes "to certain things" like cooking and cleaning, there is no compromising! A man is "the king of his castle" (as Jackie Gleason would often rant on The Honeymooners) and seeing as he "worked his ass off to pay for the maintenance for his castle, including the fresh food on the table each night—the least he was due was a hot meal and a hot bath!" When it came to the bedroom, women were expected to succumb to their husband's wishes, however strange. This common advice would prevent most husbands from "straying or growing predictably bored," at least according to my mother.

Sound advice? Who really knows for sure. Short of taking a poll or census, all we had was Mom's word. Many housewives were taught the same tactics and were subjected to the same lingo by their mothers before them. Some were lucky enough to celebrate paper, silver, and golden anniversaries with the same monogamous man. Others were on the heels of a divorce after numerous affairs tore through their happy unions like a bull in a china shop.

My sister retained her beliefs, and I retained mine. Seeing as we both are divorced, I'm not sure which of us got the better of Mom's advice!

I'm happy to admit, I still believe in Mom's reasoning. In fact, even though I'm one of those women forced to work outside the home, my "archaic or antiquated" beliefs (which I still adhere to and practice daily) are not demeaning or demoralizing. I believe women today should be much more appreciated—but at the same time, I think tradition rules in favor of Mom's way of thinking and living as far as cooking and meals are concerned. Having grown up in a household where there was always a hot, delicious meal and having been lucky enough to have been privy to Mom and Dad's affection and respect for one another, I will remain traditional in my ways as well—adhering to the adage, "If it's not broke, don't fix it!"

VINEGARED PEPPERS AND PORK CHOPS

SERVES 6

12 center-cut pork chops (8–10 pounds total)

1¾ cups vegetable oil

Salt and pepper to taste

2 garlic cloves, minced

1 cup white wine

1 cup vinegared bell peppers, with juices

1 cup hot peppers, cleaned and sliced into 1-inch pieces

1. Preheat the broiler.

2. Brush both sides of each pork chop with oil, and broil for 6 minutes on each side, seasoning with salt and pepper. Remove from the heat and set aside.

3. Heat ¾ cup of the oil in each of two skillets over high heat. To each pan add 6 pork chops, 1 garlic clove, and ½ cup wine.

4. Add ½ cup bell peppers and ½ cup hot peppers to each pan. Cover and simmer for 30 minutes, turning the pork chops frequently. Serve the pork chops hot, with the peppers scattered on top and the juices ladled over all.

ITALIAN-STYLE BROILED STEAK

SERVES 6

6 rib-eye steaks (about 6 pounds total)

½ cup olive oil

¼ cup seasoned dry bread crumbs

Salt and pepper to taste

1. Preheat the broiler. Brush both sides of the steaks with olive oil.
2. Sprinkle each side of the steaks with bread crumbs and broil for 6 minutes per side (for those who enjoy their steaks rare, broil for 5 minutes).
3. Slice the steaks diagonally into 1½-inch-thick pieces.
4. Season with salt and pepper. Serve with green vegetables and Tuscan Bread Salad (page 13).

VEAL CHOPS WITH PROSCIUTTO AND MOZZARELLA

Vitello Valdostano

SERVES 6

*Six 1½-inch-thick veal chops
(6 to 7 pounds total)*

12 slices mozzarella

12 slices prosciutto

2 cups flour

*3½ tablespoons chopped fresh
Italian parsley*

2 eggs, beaten

1 cup vegetable oil

2½ cups sliced white mushrooms

3½ tablespoons unsalted butter

3 chicken bouillon cubes

3 cups hot water

¾ cup red wine

Salt and pepper to taste

1. Butterfly each veal chop (you can ask butcher to do this when purchasing meats) and split each veal chop open like a sandwich.

2. Trim all the fat from the chops.

3. Stack the ingredients on one half of each veal chop in the following order: mozzarella, prosciutto, mozzarella, prosciutto. Using the top half of the veal chop, enclose the ingredients, sandwich-style.

4. Press down on each veal chop firmly with the palm of your hand. Place the flour and parsley together in a bowl, and the eggs in a separate bowl. Dip the stuffed chops in flour to coat, then the eggs to coat. Repeat this step (so that each chop is dipped twice in flour and egg) and set aside.

5. Heat the oil in a large skillet over medium heat. Add the veal chop stacks and fry, turning once, for about 5 minutes.

6. Remove the fried chops from the pan and place on a double layer of paper towels on a large platter to drain.

7. Add the mushrooms to the skillet and sauté for 5 minutes. Stir in the butter and return the veal chops to the pan.

8. Dissolve the chicken bouillon in the hot water, and add it to the skillet, along with the wine and salt and pepper. Bring the mixture to a boil, then reduce the heat to low. Cover and simmer for about 15 minutes, or until chops are very tender, adding additional water if the sauce gets too thick.

9. Remove from the heat and serve.

BAKED VEAL SHANK
Stinco di Vitella al Forno

3 fresh bay leaves

1 sprig fresh sage

1 sprig fresh rosemary

2 pounds veal shank, bone removed and fat trimmed (ask the butcher to do this)

Salt and pepper to taste

¼ cup flour

5 tablespoons olive oil

½ cup white wine

1 carrot, chopped

1 onion, sliced

1 celery stalk, chopped

¾ cup (6 ounces) chicken stock

2 tablespoons butter

1. Preheat the oven to 450°F.

2. Chop the bay leaves, sage, and rosemary, and rub the herbs into and outside the shank.

3. Season the outside of the shank with salt and pepper, and lay the veal shank in a shallow bowl filled with the flour. Press both sides of the shank gently into the flour to coat, and shake off any excess flour.

4. Put the oil in a roasting pan, then add the white wine, veal shank, carrot, onion, and celery. Bake the shank for 10 minutes.

5. Lower the temperature to 425°F, cover the veal shank with aluminum foil, and cook for an additional 1½ hours, basting the shank with chicken stock often.

6. Remove the shank from the pan and cut the meat into 1-inch-thick slices. Add butter to vegetable drippings in pan, and use as a gravy over the shank slices.

ITALIAN MEATLOAF
Polpe Hone

SERVES 6 TO 8

½ cup olive oil

1 cup chopped carrots

1 cup chopped celery

1 white onion, chopped

1½ tablespoons chopped fresh
  parsley

3 ounces prosciutto

1 pound ground veal

1 pound ground beef

1 beef bouillon cube

1 cup water

1 egg

½ cup flour

Salt and pepper to taste

Pinch of nutmeg

1. Preheat the oven to 350°F.

2. In a medium skillet, heat the oil and sauté the carrots, celery, onion, and parsley for 7 minutes, stirring occasionally. Remove the pan from heat and set aside.

3. Cut half of the prosciutto into small strips and mix with the ground meats in a medium mixing bowl. Knead the ingredients together until the ground meats are well mixed.

4. Dissolve the bouillon cube in the water to make broth.

5. Add the egg, flour, broth, salt and pepper, and nutmeg, and knead together to mix well.

6. Add the vegetable mixture into the meat mixture and knead well by hand.

7. Mold the mixture into a loaf and place in a 9-inch casserole pan. Place the remaining prosciutto strips across the top of the loaf. Bake for 50 minutes, or until center of meat is no longer rare. Serve with a potato dish and a green salad.

VEAL STEW WITH PEAS
Vitello alla Piselli

SERVES 6

½ cup olive oil

1 white onion, chopped

1 garlic clove, minced

1 cup chopped carrots

1 cup chopped celery

1 cup flour

2 pounds veal (for stew), cubed

1 cup dry red wine

One 8-ounce can tomato purée

1 cup cooked peas

2 fresh basil leaves

Salt and pepper to taste

1. In a large skillet over medium-high heat, heat 3 tablespoons of the olive oil. Add the onion, garlic, carrots, and celery. Cook until the vegetables are lightly browned, about 10 minutes.

2. In a medium bowl, place the flour and veal and toss to lightly coat the veal pieces.

3. Add the veal to the skillet and brown on both sides. Add the wine, cover the skillet, and cook 30 minutes or until the wine has evaporated.

4. Add the tomato purée, peas, and basil. Season the veal with salt and pepper, cover, and continue cooking on low heat (this recipe is a slow process, but be patient—it's definitely worth the wait!).

5. Add hot water as needed, as sauce may evaporate during cooking. Continue cooking for about 2 hours, or until the veal is fully cooked. Serve over rice or with crusty garlic bread.

VEGETABLE-BEEF STEW WITH POTATOES
Spezzatino Rustico

SERVES 6

½ cup vegetable oil

1 large white onion, chopped

2 pounds beef (for stew), cubed

2 cups baby carrots

2 celery stalks, chopped

1 cup fresh peas

One 28-ounce can crushed
   tomatoes, undrained

1 cup water

1 beef bouillon cube

1 teaspoon chopped fresh parsley

Salt and pepper to taste

3 large baking potatoes

1. Heat the oil in a large soup pot over medium heat. Sauté the onion until it turns translucent, then add the beef cubes and continue cooking until all sides are brown, stirring occasionally.

2. Add the carrots, celery, peas, tomatoes, water, beef bouillon, parsley, and salt and pepper. Cover the pot and let simmer for 20 minutes.

3. Peel, rinse, and cube the potatoes. Place them in a separate pot of boiling water and boil for 10 minutes, then drain the water and add the potatoes to the stew pot.

4. Cover and continue cooking for 1 hour. Serve over rice or with a piece of crusty Italian bread.

VEAL WITH HAM AND SAGE
Vitello Saltimbocca

SERVES 6 TO 8

8 veal cutlets, pounded thin (6 to 8 pounds total)

8 slices prosciutto

8 slices mozzarella cheese

8 fresh sage leaves

5 teaspoons lightly salted butter

1½ teaspoons chopped fresh parsley

Salt and pepper to taste

1. Spread out the veal cutlets. Stack 1 slice of prosciutto, 1 slice of mozzarella cheese, and 1 sage leaf on each cutlet.

2. In a large skillet over high heat, melt the butter. Add the veal slices and cook for 2 to 3 minutes. Salt and pepper to taste. Turn over once for less than a minute (cooking cheese-side down).

3. Transfer the stacks to a platter and garnish with parsley. Serve very hot (straight from the pan) for best flavor.

STEAK WITH MARINARA SAUCE
Steak Pizzaiola

SERVES 6

6 rib-eye steaks (½ inch thick,
   3 pounds total)

½ cup olive oil

One 28-ounce can crushed
   tomatoes, undrained

1 teaspoon *dried oregano*

3 fresh basil leaves

Salt and pepper to taste

1. Trim the steaks fat and any bone. In a large skillet, heat oil over medium-high heat. Add the steaks 2 to 3 at a time, browning them on both sides (approximately 2 minutes on each side). Remove the steaks from the skillet and set aside.

2. Add the tomatoes, oregano, basil, and salt and pepper to the skillet. Cover and cook for 30 minutes.

3. Reduce the heat to medium, and add the steaks to skillet, stacking if necessary. Cover and continue cooking for an additional 20 minutes.

TUSCAN BLACK PEPPER STEW
Peposo

SERVES 6

3½ pounds veal (for stew), cubed

4 garlic cloves, crushed

1¼ pounds tomatoes, diced

Pinch of salt

1½ tablespoon fresh ground
pepper, coarsely ground

1½ cups dry red wine

1. Place the meat in a large saucepan and add the garlic, tomatoes, salt, and pepper. Add enough water to cover the meat, using at least 4 cups, and cook over medium heat for 1 hour and 45 minutes, stirring occasionally.

2. When the cooking time is up, add the wine and cook for an additional 1 hour, adding additional boiling water as necessary to keep the peposo from drying out or burning. Serve hot, over either rice or noodles.

ORECCHIETTE PASTA WITH BROCCOLI RABE AND SAUSAGE

Orecchiette con i Brocoli di Rape alla Salsiccia   SERVES 4 TO 6

1 cup virgin olive oil

½ pound sweet Italian sausage links (without fennel), sliced lengthwise

4 garlic cloves, minced

1 bunch fresh broccoli rabe, stalks removed

2 chicken bouillon cubes

1 cup hot water

¼ teaspoon red pepper

Salt to taste

¼ cup grated Parmesan cheese

1 pound orecchiette (ear-shaped) pasta

1. In a medium saucepan, heat the olive oil, sausage, and garlic for about 10 minutes.

2. When the garlic has browned slightly, add the broccoli rabe and simmer for 5 to 6 minutes.

3. Dissolve the chicken bouillon in the hot water, and add it to the saucepan, along with the red pepper, salt, and 1 tablespoon of the Parmesan cheese. Cover the pot and simmer for 30 minutes, stirring occasionally.

4. In a medium pot, boil water and cook the pasta until al denté, 9 to 11 minutes. Drain it and allow it to sit in the strainer for 2 minutes (to drain any excess water).

5. Add the cooked pasta to the sausage mixture. Cook over low heat for 3 minutes, tossing the mixture repeatedly.

6. Transfer the orecchiette to a large platter and sprinkle with the remaining 3 tablespoons Parmesan cheese. Toss again and serve.

Be careful not to overcook the pasta. Al denté is a term most Italians use for the desired consistency of their pasta—firm, not mushy.

BEEF WELLINGTON

SERVES 4 TO 6

2 ready-made pie crusts

2 tablespoons olive oil

One 3½- to 4-pound filet mignon roast

¼ pound mushroom paté

Fresh parsley

Salt and pepper to taste

1. Preheat the oven to 350°F.
2. Dust a cutting board lightly with flour, and lay one pie crust on it.
3. In a large skillet, heat 1 tablespoon of the olive oil over medium heat. Brown the filet in the skillet for 2 to 3 minutes on each side.
4. Remove the roast from the skillet and place it in center the pie crust. Spread the mushroom paté evenly on all sides of the roast, excluding the bottom. For zestier flavor, spread the paté more thickly.
5. Sprinkle the parsley and salt and pepper over the roast, and lay the second pie crust on top. Wrap the sides of the pie crusts around roast, from top to bottom, pressing gently to seal the crusts together.
6. Using a cooking brush, brush the outside of the pie crusts with the remaining 1 tablespoon olive oil.
7. Place the beef Wellington in a shallow pan and bake for 20 minutes per pound (for a 3½ pound roast, bake for 70 minutes). Be sure to check your roast occasionally—about every 20 minutes or so—as oven cooking times vary. It should register 140°F on a meat thermometer when it's done. There's nothing less satisfying then an overcooked piece of meat—even if it's filet mignon! Also, each time you check your roast, baste with a hint of olive oil (this will give shine and a glistening brown color to your crust).

9

SAUCES AND SOUPS

SUNDAY SAUCES AND GARLIC SOUP

Back in the old days, Italian women were often referred to as "dowdy" or "frumpy." They were almost always in the kitchen, donned in white aprons, covered in flour and sauce patches, stirring mammoth-sized pots filled with what's commonly called "Sunday gravy." Now, before you go screaming foul or crying "uncle," you should know the women of yester-year didn't deem this task demeaning nor did they feel belittled looking/ dressing like a housekeeper and being "chained" to the kitchen stove. Cooking for their family was considered an honor as well as an art form, and whether they were considered an appropriate matriarch was judged by how contented these women kept their spouses and children at meal-time. Honest to God!

For the sake of tradition, I started learning how to cook at the age of eight. My mother propped me up on an old stepstool, stood me in front of a bubbling and battered army-sized sauce pot, and taught me the neces-sary steps to make a delicious and satisfying batch of Sunday gravy.

In my case, practice certainly made perfect—my first try was a disas-ter. Instead of stirring the tomato, basil, and meat mixture, I chose to daydream and nearly burned a perfectly good pot of sauce. The second try wasn't any better—I burned my hand instead of the sauce! Finally, on the third try, I managed to finish the long and tedious task of cutting up fresh tomatoes, frying meat cuts and fat, adding spices, and watching the clock, careful to stir the mixture every 20 minutes or so without burning anything! I can tell you it wasn't very tasty though. Thick chunks of tomato (turned a shade of shoe-leather brown from overcook-

ing) bubbled to the top of the pot—and the memory of my dad forcing himself to finish the extra-hearty portion I'd served him that Sunday afternoon will remain forever with me. Dad was so impressed with my effort, he convinced the other brave family members (including Mom) to join him at the dinner table to consume my Sunday gravy. (I'm sure my sister and brothers still hold this incident against me!)

Mom's cooking—unlike mine—always seemed perfect. Garlic soup was one of her secret cure-alls. The minute Mom heard a sniffle or saw a pair of glassy eyes at the onset of a cold, she'd whip up a batch for that night's dinner. It wasn't lobster bisque, but it truly was a good-tasting dish and seemed to actually ward off whatever ailed us. In those days, Mom's first concern was keeping us healthy. Her second concern was making sure we were clothed and warm and never went to bed hungry. That was a definite possibility, as poor as we were, but Mom and Dad constantly reminded us how much worse things could be. Both of my parents were raised amid horribly impoverished circumstances. I guess that would explain Dad's obsession with family dinners. It was the only time our entire family sat down together to eat and be thankful for all we had—and, more importantly, to bond. No matter where we were, no matter what we were doing, if we knew what was best for us, we showed up to dinner on time—no excuses—especially for Sunday dinners.

Though most people would probably consider my mother to be a more "traditional" woman than I am in some ways, my parents weren't afraid to let their amorous sides show: constant displays of affection were commonplace. I remember one Sunday dinner when Dad came down to the table earlier than usual. Before even entering the kitchen he caught a glimpse of my mother busy at work at the stove, stirring her "made with love" delicious Sunday gravy while sticking her sweat-covered face in front of the slightly cracked window in desperate need of a cool breeze. She hardly looked her best—just a hint of lip color and blush, her long, dark hair pulled severely away from her face and fastened with a silver clip behind her head. Smudges of flour, tomatoes, and splattered oil covered her apron. She looked absolutely drained—utterly exhausted at having worked nearly eight hours in the kitchen that day.

Dad, however, didn't seem to notice Mom wasn't looking her glamorous best. He stayed hidden in the shadows, some ten feet away, watching her every move. I caught him smiling, relishing the love and care she put into each recipe. Dad often bragged to anyone who'd listen about how proud he was of Mom. He respected her because she always put her family first and her children were always her priority. Mom's "old-school" ways really impressed Dad when they first met. He often told us he knew he was going to marry her the night of their first date.

Remembering the look on Dad's face that rainy Sunday evening was priceless. Later, he told me he was smiling out of pure pride at having married such a caring and giving woman.

Even years later, on his deathbed, Dad would remember what he called, "a perfect Sunday dinner"—the meal, the mood, and Mom's disheveled appearance. He insisted Mom "never looked sexier."

Here's hoping the soup and sauce recipes in this chapter do the same for you and your special someone!

SUNDAY GRAVY 1

MAKES 10 CUPS, DRAINED OF MEAT

½ cup virgin olive oil

5 garlic cloves

1 pound beef (neck bone, ribs, or other), cut into chunks

1 pound sweet Italian sausage links

1 pound pork, uncut

Four 28-ounce cans crushed tomatoes, undrained

2 tablespoons tomato paste

1 chicken bouillon cube

1 beef bouillon cube

¼ cup water

Salt and pepper to taste

4 sprigs fresh basil

½ tablespoon dried oregano flakes

½ teaspoon dried parsley flakes

1. Heat the oil in a large saucepan over medium heat. Add the garlic and brown slightly, taking care not let the garlic burn.

2. Add the meat a few pieces at a time. Brown all the pieces on both sides (about 5 minutes per side).

3. Add the tomatoes, tomato paste, bouillon cubes, and water to the meat mixture, and stir to combine. Bring the mixture to a boil and cook for 10 minutes, stirring constantly.

4. Add the salt and pepper, basil sprigs, oregano, and parsley to the pot, then cover it and let it simmer for 2 to 2½ hours, until the meat is practically falling off the bone and the sauce has thickened. Stir the pot every 20 minutes.

5. When the sauce is done and the meat is very tender, remove the meat from the sauce and set aside in a covered casserole dish. Serve both the meat and the Sunday gravy with your choice of pasta.

Remember, the longer you cook the gravy, the more flavorful it will taste. Sometimes, I cook my batch for over 3 hours—that is, if the troops aren't lining up in the kitchen with forks in their hands and growling tummies!

SUNDAY GRAVY 2 (SHORTCUT VERSION)

MAKES 10 CUPS, DRAINED OF MEAT

½ cup olive oil

2 garlic cloves, finely chopped

1 onion, sliced

3 pounds pork-based sweet Italian sausage links

Four 28-ounce cans crushed tomatoes, undrained

Salt and pepper to taste

Dash of dried oregano

2 fresh basil leaves

1 beef bouillon cube

1 chicken bouillon cube

4 tablespoon fresh Parmesan cheese

1. In a large saucepan, heat the olive oil and sauté the garlic and onion for 2 minutes, stirring occasionally to avoid burning.
2. Add the sausage and sauté for 5 minutes on each side.
3. Add the tomatoes, salt and pepper, oregano, basil, and bouillon cubes. Cover the saucepan and cook for 2 hours, stirring every 10 to 12 minutes.
4. When the tomatoes are cooked, add the Parmesan cheese. Serve over pasta.

People often ask why I have two Sunday gravy recipes. It's simple— one is faster and easier than the other. Sometimes, especially when the boys were playing Little League and most of their games were played on Sundays, I had little time to fuss and muss over my dishes. In order to make a proper, hearty, true Sunday dinner gravy, each ingredient must be properly measured and included. This shortcut variation uses only sausage as a base instead of three meats, which cuts the cooking time. But don't worry—both recipes include my secret ingredients: chicken and beef bouillon!

Whichever your preference, I'm sure your guests won't be disappointed, as both taste great!

FRESH TOMATO SAUCE
Salsa Pomodoro   SERVES 4 TO 6

6 ripe medium Roma or large
   plum tomatoes

2 tablespoons olive oil

2 cloves garlic, crushed

1 large white onion, diced

2 tablespoons chopped fresh basil

Coarsely ground salt and pepper
   to taste

1 pound fresh spaghettini or other
   thin pasta

Fresh basil leaves and/or toasted
   pine nuts (optional)

1. Blanch the tomatoes for 1 minute in boiling water, then shock them briefly in a bowl of cold water to loosen the skins. Peel and cut the tomatoes into large chunks, reserving the juice and seeds.

2. In a large skillet over medium heat, heat the oil and sauté the garlic and onion until they turn translucent, stirring to avoid burning.

3. Add the tomatoes, including the juice and seeds, as well as the chopped basil, and toss to distribute evenly. Simmer over low heat for 30 minutes to 1 hour, or until the sauce has reached the desired consistency. Remove the sauce from the heat.

4. Prepare the pasta according to the package directions and drain thoroughly.

5. Using tongs, place the pasta in the center of a serving platter pour two ladles of the salsa pomodoro on top. Keep the remainder of the salsa pomodoro simmering over very low heat on the stove, ready to use, or present it at the table in a tureen or gravy boat.

6. Garnish the dish with fresh basil leaves or pine nuts, if desired.

ITALIAN MUSHROOM SAUCE
Italiano di Funghi Porcini

¼ cup olive oil

2 tablespoons unsalted butter

1 garlic clove, minced

1 sprig fresh rosemary, chopped

1 pound fresh porcini mushrooms, stems removed and cut in slices

Salt and pepper to taste

1. Heat the oil in a large skillet over medium heat. Add the butter, and sauté the garlic and rosemary until the garlic turns translucent, or about 4 minutes.
2. Add the porcini mushrooms, and season with salt and pepper.
3. Cover the pan and reduce the heat to low. Let it simmer for 12 to 15 minutes, or until the mushrooms are tender. Serve the mushrooms and sauce immediately over fresh pasta or rice.

Fresh porcini mushrooms may be difficult to find outside of Italy but are almost always available in dried form. If you can't locate fresh porcini, mix a cup of dried porcini with fresh white button mushrooms.

MARINARA SAUCE

SERVES 6 TO 8

¼ cup olive oil

2 ounces salt pork

4 tablespoons minced onion

2 garlic cloves, chopped

Two 28-ounce cans crushed
  tomatoes, undrained

Salt to taste

6 fresh basil leaves

Pinch of dried oregano

Pepper to taste

1. Heat the oil in a large skillet over medium heat. Add the salt pork and sauté for 4 minutes, then remove and discard.
2. Add the onion and sauté until it turns translucent. Stir in the garlic and sauté for an additional minute, then add the tomatoes and salt.
3. Stir the ingredients together, cover, and allow to simmer for 1 hour.
4. Stir in the basil leaves, oregano, and pepper, and cook for an additional 5 minutes. Remove the basil leaves before using.

ITALIAN GARLIC EGG DROP SOUP

Mom's Famous Garlic Stracciatella   SERVES 6 TO 8

6 cups water

6 chicken bouillon cubes

25 cloves garlic, peeled and
    halved

2 sprigs fresh thyme

Salt and pepper to taste

1 pound fresh spinach leaves

2 to 3 tablespoons grated
    Parmesan cheese

3½ tablespoons chopped fresh
    parsley, or 1½ teaspoons dried

2 eggs

1. In a large saucepan over medium to high heat, combine the water, chicken bouillon, garlic, thyme, and salt and pepper, and bring to a rolling boil. Reduce the heat to medium and cover the pan.

2. Simmer for 15 to 20 minutes, or until the garlic is mushy.

3. Remove the soup from the heat. Remove the thyme sprigs and discard.

4. In a blender, purée the entire soup mixture in multiple batches until all the garlic has been puréed and the soup is smooth.

5. Return the soup to the pot, and place it over medium heat. Add the spinach, Parmesan cheese, and parsley. Simmer for 3 to 4 minutes, then remove from the heat.

6. Lightly beat the eggs with a whisk, and then slowly (it's necessary to do this step slowly for the proper consistency) pour them into the soup mixture, using your other hand to gently stir the soup with the whisk until egg threads form. (Alternately, you may spoon a tablespoon of the broth into the eggs and beat lightly to raise the temperature of the beaten eggs before stirring into the soup pot.)

7. Adjust the seasoning to taste, and serve immediately.

In Italian, stracciatella *means "little rag"—a fitting description because of the consistency the spinach and eggs stirred into this rich broth take on in this old-world recipe. Traditionally,* stracciatella *is made without garlic, but Mom believed—and still believes—garlic is the cure-all for anything that ails you.*

ROMAN CAULIFLOWER SOUP
Zuppa di Brocoli

SERVES 4

1 head cauliflower
4 slices white bread
2 cloves garlic
½ cup olive oil

2 tablespoons lemon juice
Salt and pepper to taste
Parmesan cheese to taste

1. Separate the cauliflower into florets. Rinse the florets thoroughly, and boil for 10 minutes in a pot of salted water. Drain the florets, reserving the cooking water.

2. Toast the bread slices. Rub each slice with garlic and place it in an individual soup bowl, discarding the used garlic.

3. After the cauliflower is cooked, pour a half ladle of the cauliflower cooking water over each slice of bread.

4. Arrange the cauliflower florets and leaves on top of the bread.

5. Drizzle the olive oil and lemon juice over each of the bowls, and season with salt and pepper. Serve hot sprinkled with Parmesan cheese.

For those of you who are wondering, brocoli *is often used in Italian to mean cauliflower. Go figure!*

WHITE WINE SOUP
Zuppa di Vino Bianco

3 cups dry white wine

2 tablespoons sugar

½ teaspoon freshly grated nutmeg

½ teaspoon ground cinnamon

¼ cup unsalted butter

3 tablespoons flour

3 cups whole milk

Salt and pepper to taste

6 egg yolks, lightly beaten

½ cup grated Parmesan cheese, optional

1. In a medium saucepan over medium-low heat, bring the wine to a slow boil. Stir in the sugar, nutmeg, and cinnamon, and continue to boil for 1 minute, then remove the pan from the heat and set aside.

2. In a deep skillet over low heat, melt the butter and stir in the flour to make a roux. Let the roux simmer vigorously until the flour turns golden, or the finished roux will taste like flour. Once the roux is golden, gradually add the milk, stirring constantly until the roux is creamy. Season with salt and pepper.

3. Pour the wine into the roux sauce, stirring until smooth.

4. Whip a tablespoon of the wine-roux mixture into the egg yolks to equalize the temperature, and then slowly pour the tempered eggs into the wine-roux, whisking all the while.

5. Remove the soup from the heat, and sprinkle with Parmesan, if desired. Ladle into individual serving bowls and serve hot.

TUSCAN VEGETABLE AND BREAD SOUP
Ribollita

SERVES 6 TO 8

1½ cups dried cannellini beans

2 garlic cloves, sliced

4 fresh sage leaves

2 tablespoons chopped fresh parsley

1 sprig fresh thyme

1 onion, sliced

2 medium carrots, diced

1 leek, sliced

12 savoy cabbage leaves, shredded

8 ounces Swiss chard, chopped

One 28-ounce can crushed Italian tomatoes, undrained

4 cherry tomatoes

1 cup olive oil

5 beef bouillon cubes

5 cups hot water

Salt to taste

½ of a 1-pound loaf sliced white bread

Pepper to taste

1. Drain and rinse the beans, and place them in a medium saucepan with the garlic and sage leaves. Cover the beans with cold water, and bring to a boil. Let the beans simmer for 20 minutes. Remove the beans from the heat and discard the garlic slices and sage leaves.

2. In a food processor or blender, purée half of the cooked beans.

3. In a large saucepan, place the parsley, thyme, onion, carrots, leek, cabbage, chard, crushed and cherry tomatoes, and ½ cup of the olive oil. Cover the pan and cook over medium heat for 10 minutes.

4. Add the whole and puréed beans to the pan, and stir the ingredients to combine.

5. Dissolve the bouillon cubes in the hot water, and pour 2½ cups of the resulting stock into the pot. Add a pinch of salt if desired, then cover

and let the mixture simmer for 1½ hours over low heat, stirring occasionally. You may add more of the remaining stock if soup becomes too thick.

6. Ladle a small amount of the soup into a large heavy saucepan, and place a slice of bread into the pan. Repeat this process until all the bread and soup are used.

7. Cover the pot and set aside for 2 to 3 hours at room temperature.

8. Return the pot to the stove over medium to high heat, and return the soup to a boil. Reduce the heat and let the mixture simmer for 20 minutes without stirring.

9. Sprinkle pepper lightly over the top of the bread and soup, and drizzle the remaining ½ cup of olive oil over all. Serve hot.

This soup needs time to develop full flavor. Make five to six hours ahead for best results.

CREAM OF ASPARAGUS SOUP
Crema di Asparagi   SERVES 4

2 pounds asparagus

¼ cup butter

1 cup flour

3 beef bouillon cubes

3 cups hot water

2 cups whole milk

Salt and pepper to taste

3 egg yolks

¾ cup grated Parmesan cheese

½ cup light cream

1. Clean and trim the ends of the asparagus stalks. Cut the asparagus into 1-inch pieces.

2. In a medium saucepan over medium heat, melt 2 tablespoons of the butter and add the flour, stirring constantly.

3. Dissolve the beef bouillon in the hot water and add it to the pan, along with the milk. Cook for 10 minutes over low heat.

4. Add the asparagus, seasoning with salt and pepper. Cover the pan and cook for an additional 15 minutes.

5. Let the pan cool for a few minutes, then transfer the asparagus and juices to a blender and purée until the mixture is smooth and consistent. Return the asparagus purée to the saucepan and place it over low heat.

6. Combine the egg yolks, remaining 2 tablespoons butter, the Parmesan cheese, and cream in a medium mixing bowl, and mix with an electric mixer on low speed until the mixture is smooth and consistent.

7. Pour the cheese mixture slowly into the asparagus saucepan, and continue cooking over low heat, stirring often, until the soup becomes thick and creamy (approximately 10 minutes). Remove from heat and ladle into individual bowls, and serve hot.

CLAM SOUP
Zuppa De Clams

SERVES 6

4 dozen small cherrystone clams

½ cup olive oil

3 garlic cloves, minced

*One 28-ounce can crushed
Italian tomatoes, undrained*

Two 8-ounce bottles clam juice

½ teaspoon dried oregano

½ cup white wine

1 teaspoon crushed red pepper

2 sprigs fresh basil

Salt and pepper to taste

Pinch of fresh parsley

1. Rinse and clean the clams under running cold water. Set the clams aside to drain and dry.
2. In a large saucepan, heat the oil over medium heat. Add the garlic and sauté for 1 minute, stirring to avoid burning.
3. Add the clams (in shells), tomatoes, clam juice, oregano, white wine, and red pepper, and stir to combine. Bring the soup to a boil.
4. Reduce the heat to medium-low and simmer for an additional 7 to 8 minutes. Cover the pan and continue to cook for another 7 minutes, or until all clams have opened up. Discard any unopened clams.
5. Stir in the basil and salt and pepper.
6. Toss with fresh parsley and serve hot in shallow soup bowls.

If you choose, you may remove the clams from their shells before serving. I prefer to keep them in, as it makes a better presentation. This dish goes well with a side of crusty, day-old Italian bread.

MAMA'S HOMEMADE CHICKEN SOUP
Zuppa di Polly Brodo

SERVES 6 TO 8

2 cups roughly chopped baby
carrots

1 cup chopped celery

1 white onion, chopped

8 cups water

1 teaspoon chopped fresh parsley

Salt and pepper to taste

1 baking potato, peeled and
cubed

8 chicken bouillon cubes

One 10-ounce can crushed
tomatoes, undrained

One ½-pound chicken breast on
bone

6 ounces orzo pasta

½ cup grated Parmesan cheese

1. In a blender, purée 1 cup of the carrots together with ½ cup of the celery, ½ of the onion, and all of the water.

2. In a large soup pot, combine the vegetable pureé, the remaining carrots, celery, and onion, as well as the parsley, salt and pepper, potato, chicken bouillon, tomatoes, and chicken breast. Cover the pot and cook for 1 hour over medium heat.

3. In a small saucepan, boil water and cook the orzo pasta for 6 to 8 minutes, or until al denté. Strain the pasta, and add it to the chicken soup. Cover and cook for an additional 30 minutes. Remove the chicken breast from the soup, and remove and discard the bone. Cut the breast meat into ½-inch pieces and return the pieces to the soup.

4. Add the Parmesan cheese to the soup, stir, and serve.

MINESTRONE SOUP
Zuppa Minestrone

SERVES 6

½ cup virgin olive oil

1 red onion, chopped

4 medium potatoes, peeled and
   cut into 1-inch cubes

2 carrots, chopped

2 celery stalks, chopped

2 medium zucchini, chopped

3 beef bouillon cubes

6 ounces cabbage

2 bundles Swiss chard
   (10 ounces total)

One 28-ounce can crushed
   tomatoes, undrained

3 fresh basil leaves

1½ tablespoon chopped fresh
   parsley

1 pound fresh cannellini beans

3 cups boiling water

12 ounces ditalini pasta

Salt and pepper to taste

½ cup grated Parmesan cheese

1 garlic clove, chopped

1. Heat the oil in a medium soup pot over medium heat, and sauté the onion until it turns translucent.
2. Add the potatoes to the onion, and sauté for 3 minutes. Add the carrots, celery, zucchini, and beef bouillon, and cook for 2 minutes, stirring frequently.
3. Cut the cabbage and chard into thin strips and add to the soup pot. Cook for 5 minutes.
4. Add the tomatoes, basil, parsley, beans, boiling water, and the uncooked pasta. Once the water starts to boil again, add the salt, pepper, Parmesan cheese, and garlic; lower the heat; and cover the pot. Simmer for 30 additional minutes, and serve hot.

ROMAN-STYLE BEEF STOCK WITH EGG

Stracciatella alla Romana

SERVES 4

Salt to taste

Pinch of freshly grated nutmeg

6 eggs, beaten

*½ cup freshly grated Parmesan
cheese*

3 cups water

7 beef bouillon cubes

1. Beat a pinch of salt and nutmeg into the eggs. Add ¼ cup of the Parmesan cheese and beat well.
2. In a medium saucepan over medium heat, bring the water to a boil. Slowly, over 1½ minutes, whisk the egg mixture into the boiling water, until the egg is set in fine threads.
3. Add the bouillon cubes, stirring to dissolve, and sprinkle with the remaining ¼ cup Parmesan cheese.

10 SIDE DISHES
SPAGHETTI ALLA "PUTTANESCA"

This side dish is a favorite of mine; I always try to have it when I visit Angelo's, an old Italian restaurant on Mulberry Street in Manhattan. It is well known for many authentic old-world-style dishes, but the puttanesca sauce is my choice when I go there.

There's actually a very funny story associated with this dish, as well. A few months ago, I was doing a press junket for Growing Up Gotti *(we were still taping the second season). The producers thought it would be cute to let my sons (then ages eighteen, seventeen, and fifteen) go to the Hamptons with a chaperone, a thirty-five-year-old family friend, Brian.*

As you can imagine, I was beside myself with worry. My sons had never spent a night away from me—and they were practically on their own, no less! The producers wanted to shoot the weekend for an upcoming episode—so, I figured with more adults there, things should go pretty smoothly.

Boy, was I ever wrong! Everything that could go wrong—did! The boys went to a teen club in Southampton, but before they left the house, I gave them a list of rules and regulations—and, of course, I reminded them that they would be punished within an inch of their lives if they disobeyed. As it turned out, it wasn't the boys I had to worry about—it was their chaperone Brian who caused all the trouble.

Because they were going to a teen club, and because they were away from home and didn't have their nagging, old-fashioned mother waiting up at the door, checking their curfew times, I assumed they would really test my patience. I called their chaperone and read him the list of "dos" and "don'ts." I instructed him that no other friends were allowed back at the house (they had three friends with them as it was) and, more importantly, no girls! At 5 A.M., I got a call from one of the producers telling me there was a girl in the house—Brian's new "side dish" (his slang for girl or "babe"). Boy, was I angry! I called Brian and read him the riot act! He was told to take the girl home immediately! He argued with me, lying and telling me the girl was actually "a friend—a long-lost childhood classmate from back in the day." Right!

I let him know he was in BIG trouble and said we would discuss this when he dropped the boys off at home. In the midst of my anger, I made a reference to his new "side dish." I let him know I didn't think too highly of any woman who would go home with a guy she just met two hours ago—and proudly parade herself half-naked in front of a half dozen teenage boys as well! I believed the word I used was puttanesca.

Well, did I hear it for that remark! Because the producers were still taping the episode, my remark was heard by a few reporters/TV critics who said I called the girl a "curse word," and said I labeled her a "whore."

Their remarks were the furthest reference from my mind. In Italian slang, the word puttanesca means "spicy" even "wild—hard to hold down."

Ever since that happened I have found myself on the receiving end of many whispers and tons of false gossip stories. While the actual meaning of the word puttana is in fact "whore," Italians (especially those raised in Italy) have always used the word as a means of saying something is hot or spicy. Of course, there are those who use the word for whore and mean exactly that, but in using slang expressions, puttana can be very misunderstood. The only way I could vindicate myself was to produce an Italian-American dictionary and show the reporters what the word really means.

SPAGHETTI WITH SPICY SEAFOOD
Spaghetti alla Puttanesca

SERVES 4

½ cup plus 1 teaspoon virgin olive oil

6 anchovy fillets, chopped

½ teaspoon finely chopped garlic

One 28-ounce can whole peeled tomatoes, undrained

Salt to taste

1 pound spaghetti or spaghettini

½ teaspoon dried oregano

2 tablespoons capers

8 to 10 black olives, pitted and sliced

1. In a large skillet over low heat, heat ½ cup of the olive oil and add the anchovies. Cook, stirring constantly, until the anchovies dissolve.

2. Add the garlic and sauté for 1 minute. Increase the heat to high and add the tomatoes and salt to taste. Bring to a boil, then reduce the heat and simmer for about 30 minutes.

3. Cook the pasta according to package directions, or until al denté, then drain.

4. Add the pasta to the sauce simmering on the stove. Add the oregano, capers, and olives.

5. Toss the pasta until thoroughly mixed, and add the remaining 1 tablespoon of oil. Transfer to a serving platter and serve hot.

STUFFED ZUCCHINI
Zucchine Ripieni

4 small zucchini, cut in halves
   lengthwise

4 tablespoons olive oil

1 small onion, diced

3 tablespoons hot water

2 eggs, beaten

½ cup freshly grated Parmesan
   cheese

3 zucchini flowers, washed and
   cut into ½-inch strips

½ teaspoon chopped fresh parsley

1 teaspoon chopped fresh thyme

1 clove garlic, minced

Salt and pepper to taste

2½ tablespoons dry Italian bread
   crumbs

1. Preheat the oven to 350°F.

2. Hollow out the zucchini halves, using a teaspoon to remove the seeds and some of the flesh. Take care that you do not puncture the skin. Chop the zucchini flesh and place it into a large mixing bowl, and set aside.

3. Heat 1 tablespoon of the olive oil in a large frying pan over medium heat, and sauté the onion until it turns translucent, stirring frequently. Add the hot water to the pan, and cook for 1 additional minute. Remove the pan from heat and set aside.

4. Combine the chopped zucchini, eggs, cheese, zucchini flowers, parsley, thyme, sautéed onions, and garlic. Season the mixture with salt and pepper, and mix well.

5. Spoon the mixture into each zucchini half and lay the halves side by side in a large casserole or baking dish. Sprinkle the zucchini with the bread crumbs and spritz with the remaining 3 tablespoons of olive oil. Bake for 15 minutes, or until lightly browned, and serve hot.

FLORENTINE-STYLE ASPARAGUS

Asparagi alla Fiorentina   SERVES 2

2 pounds asparagus   *Salt and black pepper to taste*

6 tablespoons butter   *Grated parmesan cheese to taste*

4 eggs

1. Cut and discard the bottom ½ inch of each asparagus spear.
2. Tie the asparagus stalks into bundles with 3 or 4 spears per bundle, and cook them in 1 inch of water for about 20 minutes, then drain and untie.
3. Melt the butter in a frying pan and sauté the asparagus over low heat for 5 minutes.
4. Remove the asparagus from the pan and set aside.
5. Crack the eggs into the pan, and cook on one side only (do not flip) until the yolk is no longer runny.
6. Season eggs the with salt and pepper.
7. Arrange the asparagus on 2 plates with 2 eggs atop each, and sprinkle with Parmesan cheese.

MARINATED EGGPLANT
Melanzone Marinate   SERVES 6

10 cups water

2 tablespoons salt

1 large eggplant, peeled

2 cups white wine vinegar

2½ cups olive oil

2 tablespoons finely chopped
fresh mint

2 teaspoon finely chopped fresh
oregano

4 garlic cloves, minced

Salt and freshly ground black
pepper to taste

1. In a large mixing bowl, combine 2 cups of water and the salt. Cut the eggplants into 1-inch slices and place the slices in the salted water for 1 hour.

2. In a large pasta pot, combine the remaining 8 cups of water and the wine vinegar and bring to a boil.

3. Drain the eggplant slices in a strainer, then rinse under cold water and pat dry. Add the slices to the boiling vinegar mixture, and reduce the heat to medium. Cook for 3 minutes.

4. Using a slotted spoon, transfer the eggplant slices to a double layer of paper towels. Arrange the slices in a single layer, using multiple platters if necessary, and cover with another paper towel. Let the slices drain for 1 hour.

5. Cut the eggplant slices into 1-inch cubes and transfer to a large bowl.

6. In a small bowl mix the oil, mint, oregano, and garlic, and add salt and pepper. Pour the mixture over the eggplant cubes, adding enough oil to cover the cubes.

7. Cover the bowl and refrigerate for at least 2 days to allow the eggplant to gain maximum flavor. Serve at room temperature.

This recipe is a very flavorful dish from Tuscany. In order to achieve full flavor you must marinate for at least two days.

BEANS WITH TOMATO SAUCE
Fagioli al Uccelletto   SERVES 6

½ cup olive oil

2 garlic cloves, minced

One 12-ounce can puréed tomatoes

2 fresh sage leaves

Salt and pepper to taste

One 12-ounce can cannellini beans, drained

1. In a large skillet over medium heat, heat the olive oil and sauté the garlic.
2. Add the tomatoes and sage leaves, and season with salt and pepper. Cook for 10 minutes.
3. Stir in the beans with a wooden spoon, and cover and cook for an additional 10 minutes. Serve hot. This makes a great side dish for a meat entrée such as Italian-style Broiled Steak (page 108).

SAUTÉED VEGETABLES WITH GARLIC AND OIL

½ cup virgin olive oil

3 garlic cloves, chopped

3 cups chopped vegetable(s) of
choice (broccoli, cabbage,
spinach, etc.)

Salt and pepper to taste

1. In a large saucepan, heat the olive oil and sauté the garlic until translucent.

2. Stir in the vegetables and continue cooking over medium heat for an additional 4 to 5 minutes or until desired doneness.

3. Season with salt and pepper, and serve as a side dish.

ZUCCHINI WITH PARMESAN CHEESE
Insalata di Zucchine Tenere

SERVES 4 TO 6

1 pound fresh zucchini

1¾ cups freshly grated Parmesan cheese

¼ cup olive oil

Salt and pepper to taste

Juice of 1 lemon

4 to 6 tangerine slices

1. Wash the zucchini and cut into slices ½ inch thick, and transfer to a salad bowl.
2. Sprinkle the slices with the Parmesan cheese, and toss gently with a rubber spatula to distribute the cheese.
3. In a medium mixing bowl, whisk together the oil, salt and pepper, and lemon juice.
4. Pour the lemon juice mixture over the zucchini in the salad bowl. Toss well with a rubber spatula, transfer to individual bowls, and garnish with the tangerine slices to serve.

RIGATONI PASTA WITH BROCCOLI
Rigatoni con Brocoli

SERVES 4 TO 6

½ cup olive oil

2 garlic cloves

1 bunch (1½ pounds) fresh broccoli, washed and cut into 1- to 2-inch florets

1 chicken bouillon cube

½ cup boiling water

Salt to taste

½ teaspoon red pepper

1 pound rigatoni pasta

½ cup Romano cheese

1. In a medium skillet, heat the oil over medium heat. Add the garlic and sauté until translucent, taking care not to let the garlic burn.

2. Add the broccoli to the garlic and allow to simmer for 10 minutes.

3. Dissolve the chicken bouillon in the boiling water. Add the salt, red pepper, and broth to the broccoli and simmer for another 10 minutes.

4. In a medium pot, cook the pasta in boiling water for 6 minutes, or until al denté.

5. Strain the pasta and add it to the broccoli mixture. Cook for an additional 2 to 3 minutes, stirring frequently.

6. Toss the pasta and broccoli with the Romano cheese and serve immediately.

MAMA'S ITALIAN-STYLE POTATO-EGG SALAD

SERVES 6 TO 8

6 hard-boiled eggs

6 large baking potatoes, peeled
and cut into 1-inch cubes

1 cup mayonnaise

Salt and pepper to taste

½ cup chopped fresh parsley

1 medium white onion, chopped

Pinch of cayenne pepper

1. Boil the eggs and potato cubes in large soup pot for 40 minutes; strain.
2. Run the eggs under cold water to cool, then roll the eggs on a layer of paper towels, pressing down with your palm to crack the shells and allow for easier peeling. Peel the eggs and refrigerate for 30 minutes.
3. Chop the eggs into ½-inch or smaller cubes, and fold together with the potatoes.
4. Add the mayonnaise, salt and pepper, parsley, onion, and cayenne pepper, and mix together well with a rubber spatula.
5. Chill for additional 30 minutes and serve.

HOMEMADE LINGUINE WITH RICOTTA CHEESE
Linguine e Ricotta

SERVES 4 TO 6

1 teaspoon olive oil
1 pound fresh linguine
2 cups ricotta cheese

¼ cup chopped fresh parsley
Salt and pepper to taste

1. Boil water in a large pot and add the olive oil and pasta. Cook for 6 minutes, or until al denté.
2. Strain the pasta. Add the ricotta cheese to the pasta pot and toss vigorously.
3. Add the parsley and salt and pepper, and mix well.
4. Transfer the pasta to a large saucepan over low heat, and heat the pasta for 2 minutes, tossing constantly.

ROASTED BABY POTATOES

Patate di Rustico

SERVES 6 TO 8

*18 to 20 small (1- to 1½-inch)
Red Bliss or white new
potatoes*

*1 cup coarsely chopped fresh
parsley*

5 or 6 green onions

Coarse salt and pepper to taste

*2 to 3 tablespoons olive oil (if
roasting without a meat dish)*

1. Preheat the oven to 350°F.
2. Wash the potatoes and cut in half. Pat dry with a paper towel. With a vegetable peeler or paring knife, peel each potato.
3. Remove the roots and slice the green onions into ½-inch pieces.
4. If you are roasting a meat dish at the same time (such as Beef Wellington, page 119, or Roast Leg of Lamb, page 212), during the last 30 minutes of cooking time, arrange the potatoes around the meat in the bottom of the roasting pan. Distribute parsley, onions, and salt and pepper over all.
5. If you are not roasting a meat dish, toss the potatoes in the olive oil to coat the potatoes, and place them in a foil-lined roasting pan. Top with parsley, onions, salt and pepper, and mix. Place the roasting pan in the oven and cook for 20 to 30 minutes until potatoes are lightly browned and tender.

ITALIAN-STYLE ROASTED ROSEMARY POTATOES

SERVES 6

5 large baking potatoes, peeled and cut into 1½-inch cubes

2 tablespoons olive oil

3 tablespoons dried rosemary flakes

Pinch of dried sage

Pinch of dried marjoram

Pinch of dried oregano

Salt and pepper to taste

1 teaspoon dried parsley (optional)

1. Preheat the oven to 350°F.

2. Cover the potatoes with water in a medium saucepan over medium-high heat, and cook for 15 minutes. Drain thoroughly, allowing the potato chunks to sit in the colander for approximately 10 minutes to ensure that any excess water is drained.

3. In a small roasting pan, arrange the potato chunks in a single layer. Add the olive oil and sprinkle the rosemary, sage, marjoram, oregano, and salt and pepper on top. Toss the potatoes until they are coated with the seasoning. You may also add dried parsley flakes if desired.

4. Bake in the preheated oven for 30 minutes, turning occasionally to be sure potatoes are toasted and brown on all sides. Transfer the potatoes to a flat platter and serve hot. This dish goes well with the Roast Leg of Lamb (page 212).

GRILLED ASPARAGUS VINAIGRETTE

Asparagi Vinagrette

SERVES 6

*Balsamic Vinaigrette (recipe
    follows)*

1½ pounds pencil-thin asparagus

*Olive oil or vegetable cooking
    spray*

1. Prepare the Balsamic Vinaigrette at least an hour before grilling, and set aside.

2. Break off the coarse ends of the asparagus spears. Rinse the spears and pat them dry.

3. Spray a grill pan or tabletop electric grill with vegetable cooking spray, or wipe with olive oil, and heat the grill. When the grill surface is hot, place the asparagus spears diagonally across the cooking surface to make distinctive grill marks. Cook for 2 to 3 minutes.

4. Transfer the grilled asparagus to a serving platter and drizzle the Balsamic Vinaigrette over all.

BALSAMIC VINAIGRETTE

¼ *cup olive oil*
¼ *cup water*
½ *cup balsamic vinegar*
¼ *teaspoon Dijon mustard*
1 garlic clove, finely minced
Pinch of coarse salt
Coarse pepper to taste
1 small bay leaf (fresh is preferred, dried is okay)
¼ *to* ½ *teaspoon dried tarragon*

1. Place all the ingredients into a small jar with a lid. Shake together to blend, and set aside for at least an hour before using.

2. When ready to use, remove the bay leaf and pour the dressing over the warm, grilled asparagus spears or other dish.

Note: This recipe can be easily doubled, and the dressing can be kept (in a tightly sealed jar) for up to 2 weeks.

ITALIAN-STYLE HERBED BABY CARROTS

SERVES 6

2 pounds baby carrots, peeled
¼ cup vegetable oil
1 tablespoon dried marjoram

Salt and coarsely ground black
pepper to taste

1. Preheat the oven to 350°F.
2. Fill a large saucepan with water and bring to a rolling boil. Add a few carrots at a time and blanch for 1 to 2 minutes, then transfer to a bowl of ice water. When all the carrots are blanched and shocked in cold water, drain in a colander and pat dry.
3. Spread the carrots on a baking sheet and pour the oil over all. Sprinkle with marjoram and salt and pepper, and shake the pan side to side to distribute the oil and spices.
4. Roast the carrots for 15 to 20 minutes, until lightly browned and tender. Remove from oven and place on a platter to serve.

ITALIAN-STYLE BUTTERED BABY CARROTS

SERVES 4

One 1-pound bag baby carrots
1 stick lightly salted butter

Salt and pepper to taste
¼ cup brown sugar

1. Boil the carrots in medium saucepan over medium-high heat.
2. When the carrots have cooked (about 10 minutes), run them briefly under cold running water and drain.
3. Add the butter, salt and pepper, and a pinch of brown sugar, and toss until the carrots are coated.
4. Serve on a flat platter, drizzled with melted butter and sprinkled with additional brown sugar to taste.

ITALIAN-STYLE CREAMY MASHED POTATOES

SERVE 4 TO 6

6 to 7 baking potatoes, peeled
    and cut into 1-inch cubes

Salt to taste

4 tablespoons butter

Pinch of dried parsley

Pinch of dried oregano

Salt and pepper to taste

1 cup whole milk

Fresh parsley for garnish

1. Boil the potatoes in a large pan until tender (about 20 minutes).
2. Drain the water. Transfer the potatoes to a large mixing bowl, and mash them until they are free of lumps.
3. Add the butter, dried parsley, oregano, and salt and pepper.
4. Using an electric mixer on low, whip the potatoes, adding the milk gradually to prevent splashing, until the potatoes appear creamy.
5. Garnish each serving with a sprig of fresh parsley.

ITALIAN-STYLE SAUTÉED BROCCOLI RABE

SERVES 6

½ cup extra-virgin olive oil

2 cloves garlic, minced

2 bunches fresh broccoli rabe,
  cleaned and coarsely chopped

1 chicken bouillon cube

1 cup hot water

Salt and pepper to taste

¼ teaspoon red pepper flakes

1. In a medium skillet over medium-high heat, heat the oil and sauté the garlic until it turns translucent, taking care not to let it burn.

2. Add the broccoli rabe to the skillet and sauté for 5 minutes, until the leaves become limp.

3. Dissolve the bouillon cube in the hot water and pour the liquid over the broccoli rabe. Add the salt and pepper and red pepper flakes. Stir to combine the ingredients, and cover the skillet. Cook for an additional 15 minutes, or longer if a softer consistency is desired.

SAUTÉED ESCAROLE
Scarola

SERVES 6

½ cup olive oil

3 garlic cloves, minced

2 bunches (about 2 pounds)
escarole, cleaned and roughly
chopped

Salt and pepper to taste

Dash of red pepper flakes
(optional)

1 chicken bouillon cube

1 cup hot water

1. Heat the olive oil in a medium skillet over medium-high heat. Add the garlic, and sauté until it turns translucent, taking care not to burn it. Add the escarole leaves, salt and pepper, and red pepper if desired. Cover the skillet, and cook over low heat for 5 minutes.

2. Dissolve the bouillon cube in the hot water, and add the liquid to the skillet. Cover and cook for an additional 15 minutes, stirring occasionally. Add salt and pepper.

BAKED MACARONI WITH RICOTTA CHEESE
Maccheroni al Forno   SERVES 6

1¼ ripe tomatoes

6 fresh basil leaves

Salt and pepper to taste

2 garlic cloves, chopped

1 cup fresh ricotta cheese

1 pound macaroni pasta

8 ounces Genoa salami

8 ounces provolone cheese

¼ cup olive oil

½ cup grated Parmesan cheese

1. Preheat the oven to 350°F.
2. Blanch the tomatoes by dropping them into a large pot of boiling water for 1½ minutes, then placing them under cold running water. This process will help separate the skin of the tomatoes, making them easier to peel.
3. Peel the tomatoes and cut them in half widthwise, squeezing out as many seeds as possible, then chop them roughly.
4. In a medium skillet over medium heat, mix the tomatoes, basil, salt and pepper, and garlic. Cover and cook for 30 minutes, stirring occasionally.
5. Press the ricotta through a sieve.
6. Cook the pasta in a large pot of boiling water for 3 minutes, then drain.
7. In a large mixing bowl, combine the pasta and ricotta and mix well.
8. Spread the pasta and ricotta on the bottom of a large lasagna or casserole pan. Cover with layer of tomatoes, then a layer of salami, and a layer of provolone, repeating until all ingredients are used.
9. Drizzle the casserole with the olive oil and sprinkle with Parmesan cheese.
10. Bake for 10 minutes.

RICE SALAD
Insalata di Riso

SERVES 6

2 cups water

1 cup long-grain rice

1 cup mushroom caps, brushed lightly with olive oil

½ cup pitted black olives

1 cup pitted green olives

One 6-ounce can tuna in oil, drained

1 tablespoon capers, drained

1 anchovy, chopped

½ cup olive oil

1 cup artichoke hearts in oil, drained

1 ripe beefsteak tomato, chopped

1 teaspoon chopped fresh parsley

½ lemon

4 ounces cooked ham, cut into ½-inch strips

4 ounces mozzarella cheese, cut into ½-inch strips

2 eggs, hard-boiled and quartered

1. Bring the water to a boil in a medium pot over medium-high heat, and add the rice. Cover and continue cooking over low heat for 20 to 30 minutes per package instructions. Once the water has been absorbed and the rice is soft and fluffy, remove the pot from the heat and set aside.

2. In a large mixing bowl, combine the mushrooms, green and black olives, tuna, capers, anchovy pieces, olive oil, artichoke hearts, tomato, and parsley.

3. Fold in the cooked rice, mixing well. Squeeze the lemon half over the salad to add juice, then add the ham and mozzarella strips. Garnish the salad with the egg quarters and refrigerate for at least 1 hour before serving.

In Italy, rice salad is a popular side dish, served with most any entrée, even pasta dishes.

11

DESSERTS

THE ENDS JUSTIFY THE MEANS

Italians believe in all things sweet: sweet wines, sweet sausage, sweet coffee, and sweet desserts. When it comes to food, I, like millions of others, suffer from a serious sweet tooth. In fact, at mealtimes, I find it extremely hard to restrain myself from eating my dessert before my dinner. In Italy, most Italians start their meals with a helping of something sweet—like melon or berries. These delicious, ripe fruits accompany the finest cuts of salted pork (prosciutto) and sliced cheese (mozzarella). Of course, Italians love to end their meals with something sweet as well.

No Italian cookbook would be complete without a chapter about desserts, including some of the most beloved classics like cannoli, panna cotta, and gelato (Italian ice cream).

One of my personal favorites, panna cotta, is a sweet, fluffy, and light custard. I ate so much of it growing up, I'm surprised I don't resemble a giant bowl of panna cotta! My mother used to make it twice a week because my dad and I enjoyed it so much. As a rule, Mom had a schedule when it came to cooking. She had certain recipes to be prepared on certain days, such as beef stew on Mondays, with marble cake topped with fresh whipped cream for dessert; vegetable soup and meatloaf on Tuesdays, with chocolate-banana pudding, and so on.

Panna cotta was usually served on Friday and Sunday nights. Since Mom and Dad always went out to dinner on Friday evenings (it was the only time of the week they could be alone), Mom felt guilty about leaving the kids and tried to make it easier by cooking a delicious dinner with a special dessert. We were a very close-knit family, and my brothers and sister and I whined nearly every Friday night—but when Mom would serve her incredible dessert bowls of panna cotta, it seemed a bit easier to let my parents walk out the door.

I'm not sure if this sweet Italian custard will do the trick with your little ones, but I do know they will enjoy your efforts!

COOKED CREAM
Panna Cotta

SERVES 6

3 egg whites

1 pint heavy cream

Pinch of ground cinnamon

½ teaspoon vanilla extract

Grated peel of 1 lemon

Pinch of salt

½ cup sugar

1. Preheat the oven to 175°F.
2. In a medium mixing bowl, whisk the egg whites. Stirring constantly, add the heavy cream, cinnamon, vanilla extract, lemon peel, salt, and sugar. Mix well.
3. Transfer the mixture to several individual size oven-safe ceramic dessert ramekins.
4. Bake for 40 minutes.
5. Allow the panna cotta to cool before serving—the ceramic dishes get very hot! Best served with caramel sauce.

COOKED CREAM WITH COFFEE
Panna Cotta al Caffé

SERVES 6

3 teaspoons unflavored gelatin

½ cup brewed espresso

¼ cup granulated sugar

5 cups heavy cream

2 tablespoons confectioners' sugar

Coffee beans for garnish

1. In a medium mixing bowl, combine the gelatin and espresso and let stand for 5 minutes.

2. Place the granulated sugar and 4 cups of the cream into a large saucepan over low heat, and bring to a boil, stirring often so that the cream does not scorch.

3. Remove the saucepan from the heat. Add the espresso mixture, stirring until the gelatin grains are dissolved.

4. Pour the mixture into 9-inch casserole dish and refrigerate for at least 5 hours.

5. Whip the remaining 1 cup of cream together with the confectioners' sugar until stiff peaks form. Set aside ½ cup for garnish.

6. Using a spatula, gently fold the rest of the whipped cream into the cooked cream mixture.

7. Serve cold, with the reserved whipped cream on top and sprinkled with coffee beans.

CHOCOLATE EGG CREAM
Bonet   SERVES 6

6 eggs, lightly beaten

1 cup sugar

2 tablespoon unsweetened cocoa
  powder

2 tablespoon Amaretto di
  Saronno

2 cups whole milk, heated

6 macaroons, crumbled

1. Preheat the oven to 350°F.

2. In a medium mixing bowl, add the eggs, sugar, cocoa, and Amaretto, and stir well. Add the hot milk slowly, stirring constantly. Add the macaroons, and pour the mixture into a 9-inch ring mold.

3. Place the ring mold into a large casserole pan half-filled with water, and bake for 1 hour.

4. Cool the egg cream for 30 minutes at room temperature. Remove the egg cream from the mold by gently sliding a plastic knife around the inside of the mold to loosen the edges of the bonet, then inverting the mold over a serving dish.

5. Chill the bonet in the refrigerator for 2 hours before serving.

ITALIAN CHEESECAKE
Cassata Italia

¼ cup dry bread crumbs (or substitute ready-made pie crust)

1 pound cream cheese

1 pound ricotta cheese

6 large eggs

1¼ cups granulated sugar

2 teaspoons vanilla extract

1 teaspoon freshly grated lemon peel

2 cups sour cream

2 tablespoons confectioners' sugar for garnish

1. Preheat the oven to 350°F.

2. Butter a 9-inch springform pan and coat with bread crumbs (or if using a ready-made pie crust, lay crust on bottom of the pan).

3. Combine the cream cheese and ricotta cheese in large bowl, then beat with an electric mixer set on medium until mixture is smooth (5 to 6 minutes).

4. Add the eggs one at a time, beating for 30 seconds after each addition. Fold in 1 cup of the granulated sugar, 1½ teaspoons of the vanilla extract, and the lemon peel, and beat for 4 minutes, until the mixture is creamy and uniform.

5. Pour the mixture into the prepared springform pan and bake for 50 minutes, or until the cheesecake is set in the center (a toothpick inserted in the center will come out clean). Remove from the oven, but leave the oven on.

6. In a medium mixing bowl, beat the sour cream together with the remaining ¼ cup granulated sugar and ½ teaspoon vanilla extract, and spread the mixture over the cake to coat the top.

7. Return the cake to the oven and bake for an additional 10 minutes.

8. Remove it from the oven and let cool, then sprinkle the confectioners' sugar evenly on top of the cake as garnish.

9. Refrigerate the cooled cheesecake for at least an hour, or until ready to serve.

MASCARPONE CAKE
Tiramisú

4 eggs, separated

½ cup sugar

1 pound mascarpone cheese

⅛ teaspoon salt

40 ladyfingers

1 cup brewed espresso

3 tablespoons unsweetened cocoa powder

1. Beat the egg yolks with the sugar until smooth, then add the mascarpone and blend well.

2. In a medium mixing bowl combine the egg whites and salt, and beat together until stiff peaks form.

3. Fold the egg whites gently into the mascarpone mixture, and set aside.

4. Dip each ladyfinger into the espresso and arrange them in rows on the bottom of a 9 × 13 inch glass baking dish.

5. Spoon an even layer of the mascarpone mixture over the ladyfingers, then arrange another layer of ladyfingers. Repeat this step until all the ingredients are used, ending with a layer of the mascarpone mixture.

6. Sprinkle with the cocoa powder, refrigerate for 2 hours, and serve cold.

RICOTTA PUDDING
Budino di Ricotta

½ cup raisins

½ cup semolina

12 ounces ricotta cheese

½ cup sugar

1 tablespoon finely chopped
assorted candied fruit

2 eggs

1 cup rum

Handful of dry bread crumbs

2 tablespoon butter

Pinch of vanilla sugar

1. Preheat the oven to 350°F.
2. Soak the raisins in warm water.
3. Heat ½ cup water in a small saucepan and sprinkle in the semolina, stirring constantly.
4. Allow the semolina to thicken in the saucepan. Remove the paste from the heat after 2 to 3 minutes, and spread the mixture over a wooden cutting board to cool.
5. Put the ricotta in a medium mixing bowl and stir until creamy. Mix in the sugar, candied fruit, the vanilla sugar, and 1 egg and 1 yolk, setting aside the white of the second egg. Drain the water from the raisins and add them to the ricotta mixture. Beat until smooth and creamy, then fold in the rum, mixing well.
6. Beat the remaining egg white until stiff, then fold it into the ricotta mixture.
7. Grease a pie dish using the butter and pour in the ricotta mixture. Sprinkle the bread crumb on top. Bake for 15 minutes.
8. Remove the pudding from the oven and let it cool for 30 minutes. Refrigerate the pudding for 30 minutes, and serve cold.

ITALIAN WINE PUDDING
Budino di Medici

SERVES 6

2 cups whole milk

2 ounces vinsanto (sweet Italian
    wine)

1 cup sugar

1 teaspoon vanilla

1 tablespoon honey

4 eggs

2 tablespoons black raisins

4 teaspoons pine nuts

½ cup chopped almonds

1. Preheat the oven to 350°F.
2. In a small saucepan, combine the milk, ½ cup of the sugar, vinsanto, and the vanilla, and bring to a boil. Remove the pan from the stove, and while the milk is still hot, add the honey and stir until it is completely dissolved.
3. In a medium mixing bowl, beat the eggs together with the remaining ½ cup sugar.
4. Add the milk mixture to the egg mixture and blend well.
5. Sprinkle a little sugar on bottom of a pie dish, then scatter in the raisins, pine nuts, and almonds.
6. Spoon the milk mixture into the pie dish. Bake for 50 minutes.
7. Allow the pudding to cool to room temperature, then refrigerate for 30 minutes to 1 hour.

FRIED PASTRY CAKE

Struffoli — MAKES 1 LARGE OR SEVERAL SMALL PYRAMIDS (SERVES 4)

2 cups flour
4 eggs, beaten
½ lemon
1 egg yolk
3 tablespoons unsalted butter, usually soft
Pinch of salt

1 teaspoon sugar
2 cups vegetable oil
½ cup honey
1 cup assorted candied fruit
Grated peel of 2 oranges
½ cup rainbow sprinkles

1. In a large mixing bowl, shape the flour into a mound with a deep well in the center. Pour the eggs into the well. Grate the lemon peel and add to the flour; reserve lemon.

2. Add the egg yolk, butter, salt, and sugar to the well in the flour. Using a spatula and then your hands, combine the ingredients and work into a dough ball. Wrap the dough ball in plastic wrap and refrigerate for 30 minutes.

3. Break off small chunks of the dough and roll each between the palms of your hands, forming small bread sticks 1 to 2 inches long. Repeat this process until all the dough is used.

4. Heat the oil in a large frying pan over medium-high heat, and deep-fry the bread sticks a few at a time. When the struffoli are crisp, puffy, and golden, remove them from the oil and set them on a double layer of paper towels to drain.

5. In a small saucepan over low heat, heat the honey until it is substantially thinned (but not boiling), stirring occasionally. Add the candied fruit and orange peel to the honey and stir.

6. Add a few struffoli sticks at a time into the honey in the saucepan, stirring carefully with a wooden spoon to make sure all sides are coated.

7. Remove the fried struffoli and mound them into one large or several small pyramids on piece of wax paper. Using wet hands helps with this, as the honey coating is sticky.

8. Squeeze the lemon half over the pyramid, and sprinkle it with rainbow sprinkles. Let the pyramid stand for 1 or 2 hours, then break off pieces to eat.

ITALIAN APPLE PIE
Torta di Mele

1⅔ cups flour
½ cup granulated sugar
Pinch of salt
½ cup butter
¼ cup milk

1 pound Granny Smith apples, peeled, cored, and sliced in eighths
½ cup chopped walnuts
1 teaspoon brown sugar

1. Preheat the oven to 375°F.
2. Combine the flour, sugar, and salt in a large mixing bowl. Using two knives, cut the butter into the dry ingredients until it resembles coarse crumbs. This must be done quickly, as butter melts rapidly. Add the milk a little at a time while gathering the flour mixture together with your hands until it forms a ball of dough.
3. Using a rolling pin on a lightly floured surface, roll out the dough to a ¼-inch thickness.
4. Grease a pie dish and line it with the pastry dough. Fill the pie center with the sliced apples.
5. Sprinkle the walnuts and brown sugar on top of the pie.
6. Bake for 30 minutes.

This pie tastes best when served hot, with a scoop of vanilla ice cream on top or on the side.

STRAWBERRY ICE CREAM
Gelato alla Fragola

SERVES 4

2 cups whole milk

1 cup light cream

*12 ounces strawberries, fresh or
frozen*

4 egg yolks

1 cup sugar

Fruit for garnish

1. Combine the milk and cream in a medium saucepan over medium heat. Bring the mixture to a boil for about 4 minutes, then remove it from the heat.

2. Purée the strawberries and stir into the milk mixture. Set the mixture aside to cool.

3. Whisk the egg yolks and the sugar together until creamy.

4. Stir the cooled strawberry mixture into the egg yolk mixture. Cook in the top of a double boiler for 2 to 3 minutes, then remove from heat and let it cool slightly. Pour the custard into a bowl, cover it with plastic wrap, and freeze for 3 hours. Stir the *gelato* vigorously or process it in a food processor, and return it to the freezer for another 3 hours. Alternately, an ice cream maker can be used for this step; follow the manufacturer's directions.

5. Serve garnished with fruit.

In Italy, the most popular dessert is gelato—*Italian ice cream in lemon, vanilla, coffee, strawberry, and the most favored, chocolate. It's very similar to American ice cream, except it's much creamier and even more fattening. As with most Italian recipes and foods, Italians believe the richer the better.*

DESSERTS

When I was in Italy, I was introduced to my first strawberry gelato cone in Rome on day one of the trip. That was it—I was hooked! By the last day of my vacation, I was averaging three to four gelatos a day—after lunch, dinner, and two before bedtime. The only good part of having gelato was the absence of whipped cream, chocolate syrup, and other toppings. The Italians don't believe in excess—they believe a recipe or dish should stand on its own flavor and not be altered or smothered by toppings or accompaniments that can change the overall taste. Trust me, no toppings are necessary; the gelato, like most Italian recipes and prepared foods, is delicious! I wouldn't steer you wrong on this one!

VANILLA ICE CREAM
Vanilla Gelato

SERVES 4

4 egg yolks

1 cup sugar

1 teaspoon vanilla powder
(available at specialty grocery
stores; 1 teaspoon vanilla
extract may be substituted)

1 teaspoon grated lemon peel

2 cups whole milk

1 cup crumbled vanilla wafers

1 cup light cream (if ice cream
maker is not available)

4 whole vanilla wafers, for
garnish

1. Whisk the egg yolks and sugar together in a large mixing bowl until fluffy.
2. Stir in the vanilla powder and lemon peel.
3. Whisk in the milk and crumbled vanilla wafers.
4. Finish the recipe in an ice cream maker according to the manufacturer's directions.
5. If you do not have an ice cream maker, stir the cream into the milk mixture. Cook in the top of a double boiler for 2 to 3 minutes, then remove from the heat and let it cool slightly. Pour into a bowl, cover with plastic wrap, and freeze for 3 hours. Stir the *gelato* vigorously or blend in a food processor and return it to the freezer for another 3 hours.
6. Serve garnished with a whole vanilla wafer in each bowl.

You can make this with or without an ice cream maker.
Instructions for both methods are included.

ITALIAN LEMON ICE
Granita de Limone

SERVES 4

1½ cups sugar

4 cups water

Grated peel of 3 lemons

¾ cup freshly squeezed lemon juice (4 to 6 lemons)

Lemon peel strips (optional)

1. In a medium saucepan over medium-high heat, combine the sugar, water, and grated lemon peel. Bring the mixture to a boil, stirring constantly until all the sugar is dissolved. Remove the mixture from the heat, and allow it to cool to room temperature.

2. Add the lemon juice to the cooled sugar mixture, and pour into a metal pan. Freeze for 30 minutes.

3. Stir carefully, especially the ice crystals around edges, and return the pan to the freezer. Repeat this process every 20 minutes for 2 hours.

4. Serve alone or with a garnish of lemon peel. Use an ice-cream scooper for a neater and more decorative presentation.

Another popular Italian dessert is homemade lemon ice or granita. *Most Italians love lemons. They believe the hot Mediterranean sun beams down on their gardens and makes their lemons "sing." In fact, in Italy, the lemon is probably more common than the orange is in the United States. It's a major part of the Italians' everyday diet—for instance, in Italy it's very common to see Italians walking down the street biting into a lemon sprinkled with salt for breakfast. Lemon* granita *is considered as tasty as an egg sandwich, and is eaten, scooped on a roll called a* briosia. *My favorite lemon ice recipe will delight those of you craving a light and delicious sweet dish at a meal's end.*

CANNOLI SHELLS

MAKES APPROXIMATELY 16 CANNOLI SHELLS

4 tablespoons sugar

1¾ teaspoons salt

1 cup flour

*1 tablespoon butter, softened and
cut into small pieces*

1 tablespoon dry white wine

3½ cups vegetable oil

1. Sift together the sugar, salt, and flour, the mound the combined ingredients on a cutting board. Make a well in the center of the mound, and add the butter pieces add to the center of the well. Add the wine to the well and lightly fluff the sides of the dry ingredients into the well until all the liquid has been absorbed. Knead the ingredients together by hand until the resulting dough is uniform and smooth.

2. Dust flour lightly over the cutting board and roll out the dough to a ⅛-inch thickness. Cut the dough into 3-inch squares.

3. Lay cannoli forms diagonally across the center of each square, and wrap the pastry around the forms so that the edges overlap in the center. Firmly press the overlapping corners together to seal.

4. In a medium saucepan over medium heat, heat the vegetable oil. When the temperature reaches 350°F on a candy thermometer, add the cannoli shells 4 or 5 at a time.

5. Turn the cannoli shells and cook evenly on both sides until golden and slightly blistered, or about 4 minutes per side.

6. Using a slotted spoon, remove the cannoli shells from the oil and place on a double layer of paper towels to drain any excess oil. When the shells are well drained, transfer them to a dry plate to cool.

7. Once cooled, remove the cannoli forms and fill with cannoli cream (page 184).

The most recognized Italian dessert is the cannoli. The word cannoli means "pipes" in Italian, and that's exactly what they look like. The inside filling can be altered by those with an adventurous taste palate. Some of the more common cannoli fillings are custard cream, pastry cream, chocolate cream, and my favorite, ricotta cream—it's not too sweet, not too salty, just right for my sweet tooth!

You will need cannoli forms and a candy thermometer to properly make these treats.

RICOTTA CANNOLI CREAM
Crema di Ricotta

MAKES FILLING FOR APPROXIMATELY
16 CANNOLI SHELLS

3 cups ricotta cheese

1½ cups confectioners' sugar

2 teaspoons vanilla

½ cup citron preserves

½ cup chopped candied orange peel

¼ cup semisweet chocolate chips

16 cannoli shells (page 182)

1. In a blender, blend the ricotta cheese, confectioners' sugar, and vanilla until smooth.

2. Transfer the blended cannoli cream to a bowl and stir in the citron preserves, candied orange peel, and 2 tablespoons of the chocolate chips

3. Cover the filling and chill until ready to use. The cannoli cream keeps fresh, if covered and refrigerated, for up to 3 days.

4. Fill a large pastry bag fitted with a round nozzle with the cannoli cream and squeeze mixture into the cannoli shells.

5. Decorate the cannoli ends with the remaining 2 tablespoons chocolate chips. Served chilled.

CANNOLI FRUIT PARFAIT

2 pints berries (fresh or frozen strawberries [sliced], blueberries, blackberries, and raspberries as available)

2 teaspoons superfine sugar

One 12-ounce container ricotta cheese (or mascarpone, if desired)

½ cup confectioners' sugar

1 teaspoon vanilla extract

1½ tablespoons grated orange peel

Sweetened whipped cream (optional)

1 ounce (1 square) semisweet chocolate, grated, for garnish

1. Place the berries in a bowl, and using a spatula, toss with the superfine sugar until the berries are coated. Set aside.

2. To make the cannoli cream: In a bowl with a mixer set on medium speed, whip the ricotta cheese until fluffy. Add the confectioners' sugar, vanilla extract, and orange peel, and mix well.

3. Place a spoonful of the sugar-coated berries in the bottom of a parfait glass or champagne flute. Top with a tablespoon of cannoli cream. Repeat, layering fruit and cannoli cream, until the glass is filled.

4. Top with sweetened whipped cream, if desired, and garnish with grated chocolate. Refrigerate until ready to serve.

If you have teenagers, and if you have a sweet tooth, I recommend keeping a batch of cannoli cream in the freezer for a spontaneous sugar fix. Cannoli cream will keep up to 6 months in the freezer. This simple parfait is a Sunday dinner favorite.

ALMOND BISCOTTI

MAKES ABOUT 3 DOZEN

1½ cups sugar

4 tablespoons butter

1 teaspoon vanilla extract

4 eggs

3¾ cups flour

1 tablespoon grated lemon peel

1 tablespoon grated orange peel

2 teaspoons baking powder

1 cup chopped almonds

1. Lightly grease 2 cookie sheets. Preheat the oven to 300°F.
2. In a large mixing bowl, cream together the sugar, butter, and vanilla extract with a mixer on medium speed, mixing until the ingredients are evenly distributed and look fluffy.
3. Add 3 of the eggs, one at a time, beating after each addition.
4. Add the flour, lemon and orange peels, baking powder, and almonds. Beat on low speed until a soft dough forms, then gather the dough into a ball with lightly floured hands.
5. Divide the dough into quarters. On a floured surface, shape each quarter into a log.
6. Place each log 2 inches apart on the greased cookie sheets.
7. Beat the remaining egg and brush onto the logs.
8. Bake the logs for 50 minutes. Remove from the oven and cool for 20 minutes. Leave the oven on.
9. Cut the logs into ½-inch slices, place them upright on the cookie sheets, and bake for another 20 minutes.
10. Cool at room temperature for 30 minutes.

CHOCOLATE BISCOTTI
Biscotti di Cioccolato

⅓ cup semisweet chocolate chips

1 cup packed brown sugar

2 cups flour

⅓ cup unsweetened cocoa
   powder

1½ tablespoons instant espresso
   coffee powder

Pinch of salt

1 teaspoon baking soda

1 cup chopped nuts

3 eggs

1 teaspoon vanilla extract

1. Preheat the oven to 300°F.
2. Combine ⅔ cup of the chocolate chips and the brown sugar in a food processor until the chocolate chips are thoroughly chopped.
3. In a large mixing bowl, sift together the flour, cocoa, espresso powder, salt, and baking soda. Add the processed chocolate mixture and the nuts, and mix thoroughly.
4. In a medium mixing bowl, whisk together the eggs and vanilla extract. Add this to the dry ingredients. Mix with a spatula or a blender set on low until all the ingredients form a sticky dough, then gather the dough into a ball with floured hands.
5. Divide the dough in half and roll each half into a 12-inch log. If not using the logs immediately, carefully wrap the logs in plastic and refrigerate for up to 2 days. When ready to use, unwrap the logs and place them on a baking sheet lined with parchment paper.
6. Bake the logs for 50 minutes and remove from oven. Cool for 20 minutes. Leave the oven on.
7. Peel the logs from the waxed paper and transfer to a cutting board.

8. Cut the logs into ½-inch slices, and place the slices upright on baking sheets. Bake for another 15 to 20 minutes. Allow the baked biscotti to cool to for 30 minutes, or until they are at room temperature.

9. Melt the remaining ⅓ cup chocolate chips in a double boiler over low heat, stirring constantly.

10. Place the biscotti on their sides, close together on a flat platter. Using a pastry bag fitted with a piping nozzle or a spoon, drizzle the melted chocolate over the tops. Or instead of drizzling melted chocolate over the biscotti, you can dip the biscotti into the melted chocolate, covering half of each. Cover the biscotti, making sure the covering does not touch the unset chocolate, and refrigerate until the chocolate has hardened.

These crisp, dense cookies are a favorite for coffee drinkers.
Almonds are generally preferred, but walnuts may be substituted.

ALMOND COOKIES
Amaretti Macaroons

MAKES ABOUT 2½ DOZEN

1½ cups almonds
1¼ cups confectioners' sugar

2 egg whites

1. Preheat the oven to 425°F.
2. In a food processor or blender, chop the almonds with ¼ cup of the sugar.
3. Transfer the almonds to a medium mixing bowl. Reserve ¼ cup of the confectioners' sugar, then add the remaining ¾ cup sugar and the egg whites to the almonds. Mix the ingredients by hand to form a smooth pastry mixture.
4. Roll the pastry into cylinders about 1 inch in diameter, then cut the cylinders into ¾-inch sections.
5. Roll each section into a ball by hand, and flatten each ball by pressing it gently between your palms. Arrange the cookies on a baking sheet and dust with the reserved ¼ cup confectioners' sugar.
6. Bake for 30 minutes. Allow to cool to room temperature and serve.

CREPES WITH FIGS
Crespelle con i Fichi   SERVES 4

12 fresh black figs, washed and
   quartered

2 tablespoons rum

⅓ cup confectioners' sugar

3 eggs

¾ cup flour

Dash of salt

1 tablespoon granulated sugar

1½ cups milk

¼ cup butter

1 cup heavy cream, whipped

1. Place the figs into a medium skillet and sprinkle with the rum and 2 tablespoons of the confectioners' sugar. Cover the skillet and cook over low heat for 10 minutes. Remove the fig mixture from the heat.

2. In a medium mixing bowl, beat the eggs lightly to blend. In another medium mixing bowl, combine the flour, salt, granulated sugar, and milk, whisking until the mixture is smoothly blended with no lumps.

3. Add the egg mixture to the milk mixture, mixing until the batter is smooth.

4. Grease a small skillet or crepe pan with some of the butter and heat over medium heat. Spoon in about 3 tablespoons of the crepe batter, and turn the pan so the batter spreads evenly to cover the bottom of the skillet. Once the crepe has browned, flip it over and brown the other side. Repeat this step until all of the crepe batter has been used, regreasing the skillet when necessary.

5. As each crepe is cooked, remove it from the skillet and spread some of the fig mixture over the top. Roll the crepes up loosely, with the filling inside, while still warm.

6. Sprinkle the crepes with the remaining 2 tablespoons confectioners' sugar and serve with the whipped cream.

CHOCOLATE RICE PUDDING
Riso al Cioccolato

SERVES 6

4½ cups whole milk

⅓ cup sugar

2¼ cups uncooked rice

*7 ounces semisweet chocolate
(1¼ cups chips), finely chopped*

Pinch of cinnamon

Grated peel of 1 orange

1. In a medium saucepan over low to medium heat, bring the milk and sugar to a boil, stirring constantly to avoid burning the milk. Add the rice and simmer, uncovered, stirring occasionally, for about 25 minutes, or until the rice is tender and a little thick.

2. Add ¾ cup of the chocolate and the cinnamon, and stir until the chocolate has melted. Remove the mixture from the heat and stir in the orange peel.

3. Divide the rice pudding evenly among 6 serving bowls, and sprinkle with the remaining ½ cup chocolate. Refrigerate for 2 hours, and serve cold.

TUSCAN ICE CREAM
Zuccato

SERVES 6

1 store-bought or homemade 9-inch sponge cake, divided into eighths

½ cup rum

2¼ cups heavy cream

½ cup confectioners' sugar

5 ounces bittersweet chocolate, chopped

¼ cup chopped almonds

¼ cup grated orange peel

1. Moisten both sides of the sponge cake slices with rum.

2. Line a 7-inch cake pan with the rum-soaked cake slices.

3. Using an electric mixer in a clean bowl, whip the cream until stiff peaks form, and add the confectioners' sugar. Fold in half of the chocolate, all of the almonds, and the orange peel until well mixed.

4. Melt the remaining chocolate in a double boiler, and mix in half of the cream mixture.

5. Spread the other half of the cream mixture (with no chocolate) over the sponge cake slices in the pan. Cover the pan and freeze for 15 minutes.

6. Remove the pan from the freezer. Add the other half of the cream (with chocolate) to the cake pan, then cover and freeze for an additional 4 to 5 hours before serving.

The Tuscans love cake with their ice cream. In fact, ice cream and cake are almost always served together at the end of a true Tuscan meal. Anyone with an insatiable sweet tooth can't help but applaud the combination!

CHOCOLATE SOUFFLÉ
Soufflé al Cioccolato

SERVES 4

8 ounces bittersweet chocolate

¼ cup boiling water

¾ cup sugar

6 eggs, separated

1 tablespoon butter

Whipped cream (optional)

1. Preheat the oven to 325°F.
2. Combine the chocolate and water in a medium saucepan over low heat, stirring continuously until the chocolate has melted.
3. Remove the saucepan from the heat, and stir in the sugar. Add the egg yolks one at a time, beating until they are absorbed into the mixture.
4. In a separate bowl, using an electric mixer, beat the egg whites until they form stiff peaks, then use a spatula to fold them into the chocolate mixture.
5. Butter a 1-quart soufflé pan and pour the chocolate mixture into it. Bake the soufflé for 10 minutes, then increase the temperature to 350° and bake for an additional 20 minutes.
6. Remove the soufflé from the oven, and serve hot or warm, with whipped cream, if desired.

One of my favorite desserts is a chocolate soufflé, especially after a hearty beef and potatoes meal. As a self-admitted chocoholic, I was crushed when my cardiologist (I have congenital heart disease) advised me to stay away from chocolate. Apparently, the caffeine in the chocolate does not mix well with arrhythmias. While I don't overindulge, this is the one area in which I occasionally go against my doctor's advice. Shh, don't tell anyone!

Some chocolate lovers have even equated the delicious, sweet taste of chocolate with sex—saying it's better! I'm not going to referee that debate. All I'll say is I don't know many people who would push away a piece of chocolate cake or candy. And I don't know any cooks who wouldn't jump at the chance to prepare some delectable and sinful chocolate recipe.

Chocolate soufflé has been my favorite dessert since I was a teenager. My dad took me to dinner at the Sign of the Dove in Manhattan—it was the first time I'd dined at a "real fancy" restaurant. I remember the waiters dressed all in white, including white gloves, and tending to our every need. Dessert was something of a production—especially when the staff of waiters circled our table holding huge sparklers in one hand and a trays of chocolate soufflés in the other. It was obscenely decadent!

These days, I sneak one in at every chance I can get. When I am on vacation or just traveling out of town on business, I usually call in advance and put my order in with the chef so I can guarantee the soufflé will be ready for dessert. It's one of the little luxuries I arrange for myself while on the road.

12

HOLIDAY DESSERTS

YES, VICTORIA, THERE IS A SANTA CLAUS!

One thing I am not is a stargazer. I was raised by my father to believe everyone is created equal, celebrities included. I was never so impressed by someone that I was left breathless or speechless—except, of course, the night I met George Clooney.

It was holiday time—three days before Christmas, to be exact—and of course I had waited until the last minute to go shopping. I left my office at the New York Post at 6:00 sharp and did my best to get uptown to 50th and 5th by 6:30 P.M. Bergdorf's was open until 9:00 and I was confident I could somehow grab all thirty-two gifts on my list in less than two hours—including having them expertly wrapped.

Talk about wishful thinking! By 8:15, I was all shopped out, thoroughly exhausted as I pushed my way through the crowd, past numerous window displays to an alcove covered with tiny, bright Christmas lights, and crowded with what seemed like thousands of blonde and brunette elves, dressed in faux attack gear. Each was armed with test vials of choking perfumes and toilet waters, aimed at the oncoming phalanx of shoppers heading their way.

"Please try this," said one very pushy nineteen-year-old with a maniacal smile.

"You have to try this," shouted another red-clad ingénue, this one a pesky brunette.

The third woman dressed as an elf, an overly made-up redhead, didn't bother with niceties at all. She just ran up to me, pulled out a small glass bottle of amber liquid, and spritzed away, smacking me dead on in my face.

My eyes felt like they had tiny pins with fire sticking in them. Tears streamed down both cheeks. I groped blindly for a tissue, relying on memory to find the delicate silver-plated tissue holder atop the MAC Cosmetics counter to my left, all the while coughing and choking as the caustic, vile-tasting liquid slithered down my throat.

As for my assailant, she never even bothered to help me. Instead, she did an about-face and headed toward her next unsuspecting victim, who unfortunately turned out to be a little old lady, wrapped in a black cashmere shawl and clutching a worn black umbrella under her left arm.

After the sudden perfume attack, I was no longer in the holiday shopping mood. I grabbed my pal Jake's arm (I had persuaded him to come along to help me haul my packages) and beat a hasty retreat to the 59th Street exit.

Outside, a light snow had begun to fall and a gust of icy wind slapped me hard in the face, leaving me with red, rosy cheeks to complement my already irritated and chemical-sensitive skin. I didn't have to look in the mirror to know I looked like one big cherry jelly bean. I stood at the curb to flag a passing taxi but before I had a chance to raise my right arm in that New York cab-hailing ritual, I heard people shouting my name.

"Victoria, can you look to the right?"

Then another voice, "Ms. Gotti, over here please."

There was a mob of reporters, photographers, and cameramen, crowding the entrance of the Paris Theatre, adjacent to Bergdorf's—and it was charging my way, tripping over one another for front row placement. I looked up at the theater marquee overhead and with burning red peepers saw George Clooney's name in bright lights, and underneath it: Confessions of a Dangerous Mind.

It was the New York premiere of the film about game show host Chuck Barris's life, starring, and produced by, Clooney. I had heard the hype, read all the gossip, even seen the preview. In fact, the invitation to *the New York premiere was sitting on my desk in my office, in my "events to get to" file.*

Obviously, I'd forgotten the premiere was tonight. In what seemed like a split second, I was standing in front of the cameras, a microphone aimed at my face, and, as flashbulbs popped in the background, I was asked, "Why did you come out to support George tonight, Victoria?"

Before I could answer, Miramax honcho Harvey Weinstein stepped out of a shining limo and headed in my direction. "Hello, Victoria! Thanks for coming," he waved and yelled, "See you inside."

So it looked like I'd be going to the screening after all. I knew I looked a sight—dressed in my usual work uniform of black Armani slacks, a matching fitted blazer, and what started out as a clean, crisp-collared white shirt—and oh, did I mention a pair of comfortable, office-only flats? You get the picture. I wasn't exactly glammed up for a movie pre- miere. What a time to be surprised standing in front of the Paris Theatre, clutching a mountain of Bergdorf shopping bags in assorted sizes—and did I mention my red face?

While I'm sure I managed to conceal my embarrassment well with a bright smile and the usual Miss America hello (wrist bent up, open hand moving from left to right), my words gave me away. When I answered the journalist's question, it was as if I was an automaton, and speaking in slow motion. "I'm here to support my future husband, George."

In an instant, the cacophony of reporters and fans' voices ceased. A silent hush fell over the crowd. I remember the journalist's expression of shock and intense curiosity, and then shock again when I murmured, "Oh, George doesn't know yet, but we're getting married."

Immediately after, everything else was a blur—somehow I managed to get inside the theater and get to my seat, watch the movie for two and a half hours, even hop a cab to the premiere's after-party at the W Hotel in Times Square, all on automatic pilot. I was no longer overcome by ex- haustion brought on by my intense shop-a-thon and perfume assault and the subsequent shock at having been thrust smack down into the center of a major movie premiere.

By now I was nearly catatonic over the stupid Clooney husband remark, a classic case of "oops, did I say that out loud?" knowing full well my remarks would make headlines on page six, and Rush and Malloy tomorrow. And that's not to mention half a dozen other publications and the on-camera interview I did for Entertainment Tonight.

I managed to find an empty, quiet corner, somewhere in the back of the ballroom reserved by Miramax for the sole purpose of Clooney's post-premiere party. Because I was so well hidden, few people stopped to talk to me, with the exception of an old P.R. pal, Sam, now a top-level publicist at Miramax. She casually reminded me that my stupid remark was sure to create a press frenzy. Then, as a by-the-way, she mentioned that Clooney was a fan of mine as well, and that he wanted to meet me.

Perhaps it was the shock of learning that Clooney even knew I existed or just my imaginative nature thinking I actually had a chance with George—but I smiled from ear to ear. I was still embarrassed, mind you, but happy with excitement nonetheless.

Immediately I launched into Holly Golightly mode, Audrey Hepburn's character in Breakfast at Tiffany's. Gone was the anxiety-provoking panic attack, the quick and labored breaths, sweaty palms, and intense desire for the floor to open up and suck me downward. I was suddenly exuding self-confidence—even my red face seemed to disappear all at once.

Before I could open my mouth to question Sam further, George Clooney appeared, looking every bit the handsome, charismatic Hollywood leading man he is. He smiled warmly and took my hand. I almost fainted!

"So you are the Victoria Gotti," he said, more than asked.

Compared to his cool, calm, and collected presence, I was a trembling, shaking basket case. Clooney brushed the lapel of his dark, expensive suit jacket, then asked, very matter-of-factly, "How are you?"

I should have apologized for my casual appearance, even bored him with my Christmas shopping fiasco, explained about my red face and, of course, my stupid husband comment, but I was frozen. My legs were like blocks of concrete embedded in the floor and, suddenly, I was mute.

I did manage a half "I'm so nervous I could die" smile and a nod.

Even when he said, "I'm a big fan of your work, your novels," I still found it difficult to speak. Here was George Clooney, standing before me, looking like Mr. Perfect, admitting that he was a fan of my work, and all I could manage was a half smile and a nod.

I'm sure he could sense my nervousness. At least I hoped so; otherwise, he'd deem me unsociable and snobby, but he definitely realized that the conversation between us was one-sided so he beat a hasty retreat to the VIP section of the room reserved for Clooney and his close pals. Of course he invited us to join him, and of course I declined.

The moment Clooney was out of earshot, I all but tackled a passing waitress holding a tray of stuffed miniature artichokes. I grabbed a handful and stuffed as many as I could fit into my mouth. I'd read somewhere that Clooney loved stuffed artichokes. How ironic, I thought. I'd also read somewhere that he loved Italian food, and that his aunt, Rosemary Clooney, who was quite the cook, used to prepare George's favorite Italian dishes while waltzing around the kitchen belting out some of her hit tunes, classics like "Mambo Italiano" and "Pretend You Don't See Her." In fact, Clooney loves the Italian culture so much he recently bought a villa near Lake Como and spends all of his free time wandering the Italian villages, towns, and countryside.

Arrgh! Mr. Perfect was becoming more and more perfect. Too bad I made a colossal fool of myself when we met. It was nearly 11:00 when I decided to leave. I walked discreetly to the hotel's 49th Street exit, but before pushing open the door, I spotted the waitress with the artichokes and grabbed another handful for my ride home.

The next day, as predicted, my Clooney remark was everywhere, including the New York Times! Oh, how embarrassing!

I stayed in bed for two days with the covers over my head. No phone calls; no visitors. I wouldn't even come downstairs for dinner. I figured by day three it would be yesterday's news, so I ordered in an Italian feast. I had a healthy portion of baked ziti, a side of three meatballs, and a delectable and healthy serving (or two or three) of Bergdorf's famous fruitcake, and, of course, stuffed artichokes as my appetizer. I dined in private while watching my own George Clooney film festival: From Dusk Til Dawn, One Fine Day, and Irreconcilable Differences.

Unlike Michelle Pfeiffer, I may not have landed the gorgeous leading man in the end—but I did adjust my wish list to Santa to include someone "tall, dark, and handsome." Hey, at holiday time a girl can dream, can't she?

CHRISTMAS PIE

Spongata   SERVES 6

½ cup golden raisins

1 cup unflavored dry bread
   crumbs

1 cup strawberry jam

1 cup finely chopped walnuts

1¾ cups honey

½ cup water

½ cup pine nuts

Pinch of cinnamon

2½ cups flour

½ cup granulated sugar

Pinch of salt

Grated peel of 1 lemon

¾ cup butter

2 eggs

2 egg yolks

Dash of confectioners' sugar

1. Preheat the oven to 375°F. Soak the raisins in water for 1 hour, then drain.
2. Spread the bread crumbs on a baking sheet lined with aluminum foil, and place in the oven for 8 minutes to brown slightly. After toasting, transfer the bread crumbs to a mixing bowl and add the jam and walnuts.
3. In a small saucepan over medium heat, heat the honey and water, and cook until boiling, stirring constantly.
4. Stir the honey mixture into the bread crumb mixture, and add the raisins, pine nuts, and cinnamon. Using a spatula, mix well. Cover the bowl and refrigerate for 2 days.
5. Preheat the oven to 375°F.
6. In a separate mixing bowl, sift together the flour, granulated sugar, salt, and lemon peel, and mix well.
7. Cut the butter into the flour mixture using two knives moving in an outward pulling direction. Repeat this action until the mixture looks like bread crumbs.

8. Add the eggs and egg yolks, and mix well. Using your hands, knead the mixture into a dough and form a ball. Wrap the dough ball in plastic wrap, and refrigerate for 1½ hours.

9. Roll half of the dough into a ball and flattened slightly to a disk shape, and place it on a lightly floured cutting board. Using a rolling pin, roll out the dough to a ⅓-inch thickness. Using an 11-inch pot lid or a pie tin overturned onto the dough, trim a neat circle out of the dough.

10. Repeat step 9 with the other half of the dough, this time trimming it into a disk about 9 inches across.

11. Transfer the smaller dough round to a sheet of baking paper laid atop a cookie sheet. Spoon the honey filling evenly onto the round, leaving a space of about ½ inch around the edges.

12. Lay the larger dough round on top of the filling, and, using your fingers, pinch down on the edges to seal the crusts together. You may use the tines of a fork to make decorative markings around the circumference of the disk.

13. Bake the pie for 25 to 30 minutes, or until it is slightly golden brown. Remove the pie, let it cool, and then spinkle with confectioners' sugar.

You need to plan ahead for this pie. The filling needs to "cure" for two days before the spongata *is assembled.*

NEAPOLITAN CHRISTMAS FRITTERS
Neapolitan Struffoli

SERVES 10 TO 12

3½ cups flour

4 eggs

2 tablespoons sugar

½ cup anise liqueur

Pinch of salt

2 cups vegetable oil

¾ cup honey

1 cup chopped candied orange

1 cup diced candied lemon peel

¾ cup heavy cream

¼ cup rainbow sprinkles

1. In a medium mixing bowl, combine the flour, eggs, sugar, liqueur, and salt, and beat until the mixture is thick, then use your hands to knead it into a dough. Set the dough aside for 2 hours.

2. Scoop out spoonfuls of the dough by the tablespoon, and roll each spoonful into a small ball.

3. Heat the oil over medium heat in a large frying pan. When the oil is hot, fry the dough balls in batches until all the dough mixture is used. Cook for about 1 minute or until golden.

4. Scoop the *struffoli* out of the oil with a slotted spoon to avoid being burned, then place them on a double layer of paper towels to drain and dry.

5. Heat the honey in a large saucepan over low heat until it is substantially thinned (but boiling), then stir in the candied orange and lemon peel.

6. Add the *struffoli* a few balls at a time to the honey and stir gently and thoroughly with a wooden spoon, until all the dough balls are coated with honey and fruit.

7. As each batch of *struffoli* is coated with honey, remove it to a serving

platter using a wooden spoon. With wet hands, arrange the *struffoli* in a pyramid and decorate with the sprinkles.

8. Allow the *struffoli* pyramid to cool and harden for about an hour. When ready to eat, simply break off pieces of the struffoli as desired.

Neapolitan struffoli *is one of my favorite holiday dishes. I start making my batches in early December, and my kids, their friends, and random company devour the* struffoli *by the handfuls! Not only is the sweet dessert delicious, but the tiny, sprinkle-covered fried dough balls look as pretty as a Christmas tree decoration. Every year when I whip up a batch, it signals that holiday season has officially begun!*

Of course, struffoli *is not only meant to be enjoyed at holiday time. This snack/dessert is so tempting and pretty, I tend to eat half a pyramid myself!*

CHRISTMAS EVE CAKE
Dolce di Natale   SERVES 8

½ cup raisins

1½ cups warm water

13 dried figs, stemmed and
   chopped

1 cup chopped walnuts

⅔ cup pine nuts

1 tablespoon grated orange peel

6 tablespoons grappa (Italian
   brandy)

3⅔ cups flour

2 teaspoons baking powder

¼ teaspoon salt

½ cup unsalted butter

¾ cup sugar

3 eggs

¼ cup whole milk

1. In a medium mixing bowl, soak the raisins in the warm water for 10
   minutes.
2. Drain the raisins, then add the figs, walnuts, pine nuts, orange peel,
   and grappa. Cover the bowl and set aside for 30 minutes.
3. Preheat the oven to 375°F.
4. In a large mixing bowl, sift together the flour, baking powder, and salt,
   and set aside.
5. In a medium mixing bowl, combine the butter and sugar, beating until
   creamy. Beat in the eggs then fold in the dry ingredients. Stir in the
   milk and beat until the mixture in the bowl becomes a smooth batter.
   Fold their nut mixture.
6. Transfer the batter to a 9-inch round cake pan, and bake for about 1 hour,
   or until a knife inserted into the center of the cake comes out clean.
7. After letting the cake cool, remove it from the pan by sliding a knife
   around the edges to loosen it, upending it over a plate, and gently tap-
   ping the bottom of the cake pan until the cake slides loose. Serve the
   cake at room temperature.

13

SUNDAY DINNERS

SAUCE IN STILETTOS

Sunday dinner these days generally means restaurant reservations, and only for planned celebrations like bridal and baby showers, birthdays, and traditional holidays like Mother's Day and Easter. Blame it on dual-career households and the fast pace of overscheduled kids' weekend activities, or simply the need for socialization for harried moms in need of a day of R&R. Gone are those traditional family gatherings, when Sunday dinner meant donning your Sunday best, attending 10:00 mass and experiencing the comforting sight of your mother, aunts, and neighbors hard at work in preparation for the usual weekly feast.

In my parents' household, dinnertime was important. Chalk it up to nostalgia or tradition, but my father was a stickler for family time. In his words, it was bad enough women were "forced to work because of a compromised economy, divorce, single parenthood, and other extenuating circumstances." As he saw it, in a gentler world, a child's only responsibility was to be a good student—absent were after-school jobs and activities. And moms would remain the caregivers or Florence Nightingales of the household, responsible for the well-being of their young ones and their spouses. That included preparing well-balanced meals, no matter your financial bracket.

Whether you could afford filet mignon or ground beef, beluga caviar or deviled eggs, you could eat well. The simplest, least expensive ingredients, like a fresh bunch of escarole that cost pennies, could easily be transformed into a hearty, delicious meal with Mom's culinary skills and creativity.

At our house, you were expected to sit down at the dinner table, well dressed and well groomed—hair neatly combed, hands and face scrubbed, shoes polished and free of scuffs. And Sunday dinners were even stricter!

This weekly ritual continued well after I left home. I was a wife and mother with three babies toddling about, running a household and taking care of all the errands—and oh, yes, I had a day job running my own women's clothing company. My husband, babies, and I still had to be at Sunday dinner at my parents' house, on time and looking our best, Sunday after Sunday.

Maybe it seemed far too traditional to me back then, as I am sure I protested more than once, but it is a tradition I chose to take with me as my own children grew—one I am most thankful for. No matter how hectic my work week is, no matter how busy my children are, we have a definite standing dinner date come Sunday. We feast on a meal made with love and we trade stories with each other, laughing, talking, and offering advice.

The importance of keeping your family close-knit in today's relaxed and mobile society is very, very important and necessary! In order to remain current and up to date in your children's lives—what they're doing and who they're doing it with—you need to be involved in their conversations and activities at least weekly. Besides, letting your family know just how much you love and adore them by putting the extra effort into a carefully planned and cooked homemade meal on Sunday is the least you can do as the matriarch—a title moms have rightfully earned. In busy households where moms are working full-time and the kids are preoccupied with after-school work and activities, friends, and hanging out at the mall, Sunday dinner should represent "formal family time" with everyone in attendance, looking their best. Bragging rights (like a recent salary raise or an A in mathematics) and boastful tales of achievement take the place of ordinary, loving conversation.

Trust me, even the most hectic, on-the-go household Sunday dinners will become an event most enjoyed and anticipated come the beginning of every mundane Monday!

MOM'S MEATBALLS

MAKES ABOUT 2 DOZEN MEATBALLS

1 pound ground beef

1 pound ground veal

½ pound ground pork

2 tablespoon grated Parmesan
   cheese

2 eggs

3 garlic cloves, minced

Salt and pepper to taste

2 tablespoon raisins

2 cups warm water

Half a ½-pound loaf stale (1 to 2
   days old) Italian bread

2 tablespoons olive oil

1. In a large mixing bowl, combine the ground meats, grated cheese, eggs, garlic, salt and pepper, and raisins. Knead the mixture by hand to combine thoroughly.

2. Pour the warm water into a medium mixing bowl, and break the Italian bread into 3 pieces and soak for 5 minutes.

3. Drain and gently squeeze excess water from the bread.

4. Fold the wet bread into the ground meat mixture, kneading until all ingredients are well combined and the bread has a mushy consistency.

5. Mold the meat and bread mixture into small (2-inch) balls, rolling the balls between your palms for the best shape.

6. In a large frying pan, heat the oil and add the meatballs, covering the pan to help meatballs to cook more quickly. Continue cooking until the middle of the meatballs are no longer pink, turning meatballs with a wooden spoon occasionally until done, about 8 minutes.

PAPPARDELLE WITH HOT SAUSAGE SAUCE

SERVES 6 AS AN APPETIZER OR 4 AS A MAIN COURSE

*½ pound hot Italian sausage
  links*

½ cup extra-virgin olive oil

1 cup chopped onion

1 cup dry white wine

*Two 28-ounce cans crushed
  Italian tomatoes, undrained*

Salt to taste

Pinch of dried oregano

Black pepper to taste

6 fresh basil leaves

*1 pound pappardelle noodles (use
  fresh pasta if possible)*

*3 tablespoons freshly grated
  Parmesan cheese*

1. Chop the sausages, breaking the meat into crouton-size chunks, and set aside.

2. Heat the oil in a large skillet over medium to high heat. Sauté the onion for about 3½ minutes, stirring occasionally, or until the onion turns translucent. Stir in the sausage meat and sauté for about 6 minutes, or until the sausage is thoroughly cooked. Drain the excess fat from the skillet.

3. Add the white wine, stirring constantly, and increase the heat to high. Bring the mixture to a boil for about 3 minutes.

4. Add the tomatoes and salt. Cover the skillet and let the mixture return to a boil. Simmer at a reduced heat for about 20 minutes, until sauce has thickened.

5. Stir in the oregano, pepper, and basil. Add extra salt and pepper if necessary.

6. While the sauce is cooking, cook the pasta according to the package directions, or until al denté, taking care to add a pinch of salt into boiling water. Drain the pasta once cooked.

7. Return the drained pasta to the pot. Over medium heat, stir in 1 cup of the sausage sauce and toss together.

8. Remove the pasta from the heat. Transfer it to a large serving platter and spoon the remaining sauce over the top. Sprinkle the top with grated cheese to taste.

ROAST LEG OF LAMB
Abbacchio Al Forno

SERVES 6

One 6- to 7-pound leg of lamb
Salt and pepper to taste
1 tablespoon dried rosemary
1½ cups extra-virgin olive oil
2 onions, chopped
2 cups chopped celery
2 cups baby carrots

3 tablespoons flour
1 cup dry white wine
2 cups water
2 chicken bouillon cubes
One 28-ounce can crushed
  tomatoes, undrained

1. Preheat the oven to 375°F.
2. Trim any excess fat from the leg of lamb. Season the lamb with salt and pepper and rosemary, rubbing the seasonings by hand into all the surfaces and crevices.
3. Heat the olive oil over medium heat in a medium roasting pan or Dutch oven. Place the seasoned roast in the pan, cover loosely with aluminum foil, and roast for 30 minutes.
4. Remove the pan from the oven and add the onions, celery, and carrots. Bake covered for another 25 minutes, or until the vegetables are lightly browned.
5. Remove the pan from the oven, and transfer the roast to a warm plate.
6. Drain all the excess fat and oil from the vegetables, then return them to the pan. Add the flour and toss the vegetables gently until they are coated. Add the white wine, water, bouillon cubes, and tomatoes, and mix well.
7. Return the roast to the vegetables in the pan and bake covered, for an additional 30 minutes, or until a meat thermometer registers 155°F.

8. Transfer the meat to a serving platter and allow to rest for 20 minutes before carving. Using a slotted spoon, place the vegetables into a bowl or arrange on the platter around the roast as desired.

9. Pour the residual vegetable and meat juices into a medium saucepan and place it over medium heat, stirring and adding salt and pepper. Bring the gravy to a boil, then remove from the heat and serve over the meat.

This dish goes well with the Italian-style Roasted Rosemary Potatoes (page 155) and the gravy on the side.

SUNDAY LASAGNA

SERVES 6 TO 8

2 pounds ricotta cheese

1 pound shredded mozzarella

1 cup freshly grated Pecorino Romano cheese

2 eggs, beaten

½ cup milk

Salt and pepper to taste

½ cup plus 2 tablespoons extra-virgin olive oil

1 cup finely chopped onion

3 garlic cloves, minced

2 pounds sweet Italian sausage (removed from casing and chopped)

2 quarts Sunday Gravy (page 124 or 126)

1½ pounds lasagna noodles

Dried oregano and parsley flakes to taste

1. In a large mixing bowl, combine the ricotta, ¾ pound of the mozzarella, ¾ cup of the Pecorino Romano cheese, the eggs, milk, and salt and pepper. Whisk the mixture by hand until it looks creamy and the ingredients are evenly blended. Cover and refrigerate the mixture for 1 hour.

2. Heat ½ cup of the oil in a large skillet over medium heat. Add the onion, garlic, and sausage. Sauté for 6 minutes, stirring occasionally to avoid sticking.

3. In a large saucepan, heat the Sunday gravy. Stir in the sausage mixture, and add salt and pepper as desired. Cover the saucepan and simmer over low heat, stirring occasionally, for 10 minutes.

4. Preheat the oven to 350°F.

5. In a large pot filled with boiling water, place the lasagna noodles and the remaining 2 tablespoons of olive oil. Cook the noodles until al

denté, typically 6 to 8 minutes. Drain the noodles, then run each piece under cold water and set aside.

6. Spread a thin layer of the Sunday gravy on the bottom of a lasagna pan, and place a single layer of noodles on top of the sauce.

7. Top the noodles with another ladle of gravy.

8. Drain any excess liquid from the refrigerated ricotta mixture, and spoon ¼ of the mixture over the first layer of noodles and sauce. Repeat this process three times, layering noodles, Sunday gravy, and cheese four times (there should be four layers in total), and end with a layer of the Sunday gravy. Sprinkle the remaining mozzarella and ¼ cup Pecorino Romano on top of the lasagna, and sprinkle with oregano and parsley flakes as desired.

9. Bake the lasagna for 40 minutes, or until the cheese on top is golden and bubbling.

10. Allow the lasagna to cool for 30 minutes before serving.

In my family, I am most praised as a cook for my lasagna, generally reserved for holidays, like Easter, Christmas, and even Mother's Day. Using one or two secret ingredients, my recipe deviates just a pinch from the norm. I urge all to try it. You'll get rave reviews, I promise!

One year, just before Christmas, I had heart surgery—nothing major, as far as I was concerned—just a necessary "tune-up." I bounced back fairly well, but not 100 percent. My brother John, concerned I wasn't up to hosting the usual Christmas celebration, decided to cater Christmas dinner with food from a local Italian restaurant. I wasn't happy about it; in fact, I told him I was still going to make some of my most requested dishes. I'm not sure how our wires got crossed, but my brother assumed I meant my famous, much-asked-for lasagna as well. Being a bit fatigued and feeling sluggish in the kitchen, I decided that John was right and I'd leave the heavy work to the caterers.

Imagine the disappointment when everyone, who'd been anticipating my holiday lasagna, realized I didn't make it that year! Ever since then, every Christmas, my siblings call me up on December 23 to make sure I haven't forgotten the lasagna!

My siblings aren't the only ones in the family who love my lasagna. Once, while visiting Dad in prison, he brought up the old days and our holiday meals. We laughed and laughed. Then Dad turned to me and said, "What I wouldn't give for a plate of your homemade lasagna now."

He said he'd gotten pretty spoiled having pasta and Sunday gravy every week for years, and now, he missed it terribly. I believe he said something like, "I would give my right arm just to taste a plate of homemade pasta—just a taste."

I felt sorry for him—and realized just how important Sunday dinners and Sunday sauce really was. After that day, I never took those "annoying family gatherings" for granted again—nor a bowl of fresh-made pasta or a plate of homemade lasagna. Each time I take a forkful, I remember the wistful expression on his face and the sparkle in his eyes, and I appreciate the dish all the more.

14 ⚬⚬

MENUS

As you've probably gathered already, food plays a major part in the daily life at the Gotti home, and it's not just because I have three teenage sons. I find the preparation of good food to be extremely relaxing and serving delicious meals to friends and loved ones a genuine expression of love. By now, I've planned, prepared, and hosted so many dinner parties, presided over so many family gatherings, and entertained so many friends at bridal showers, I no longer fret over what to serve.

Never take for granted that you'll be able to meet the dietary requirements of all of your guests every time you host a dinner party. With so many people on diets (not just the overweight but those who only think they're overweight) religiously following the Atkins, Zone, South Beach, and Weight Watchers menus, not to mention environmental and animal rights activists who refuse to eat "food with faces" or whatever the endangered dish du jour might be—it's becoming increasingly difficult to please everyone.

Constructing a menu that's acceptable to all is the hardest part of planning a dinner party, not to mention hosting it. I've learned through trial and error that a good piece of fresh fish is often a safe bet, as is chicken. Despite the popularity of no/low-carb diets, the days are long gone when a juicy, tender cut of beef was considered a delicious sign of hospitality. So what's a hostess to do?

As a self-admitted homebody, I've become quite accustomed to entertaining in my home, inviting those I know and those I'd like to know better into my sanctuary to feast on a labor of love, especially designed, prepared, and created by moi. I treat such occasions as celebrations for favorable events—like landing a new job.

A few years ago, while working at Star, a popular tabloid magazine, I was promoted to executive editor at large, besides being the magazine's number one celebrity reporter. (I'd been bringing in the cover story week after week for several months.) My new position and hefty raise was brought about by the company's hiring a new editorial director. What better way to celebrate two such notable and worthy occasions than an elegant dinner party at home?

Since it was late May and spring was blooming everywhere with warm air and sprays of colorful flowers sprouting about the grounds, I decided to make the dinner an elegant al fresco experience.

Whether you have a 4- by 5-foot terrace or a spacious quarter-acre patio, nothing complements good food and great conversation better than beautiful spring weather, breezes laced with the scent of flowers, and nature's nighttime sounds providing the perfect soundtrack.

I had less than a week to prepare, so I made my list of guests and tasks, saving the menu for last. I called the party store and placed my order for three large round tables and thirty white ballroom chairs, as well as three antique white linen tablecloths and sterling silver candelabras. Loving fresh flowers as I do, I decided to make the four or five centerpieces myself. So I ordered a hundred cream and pink tea roses and a few bunches of baby's breath and fern leaves to fill out my arrays from a flower wholesale outlet I came across on the Internet. The cost was a mere fifty cents a rose. Compared to other florists who charge an average five dollars a stem, I'd gotten an incredible bargain!

The morning of the party, I set up the tables with white wooden chairs and ten place settings each out on the terrace, draping each table with white linen and lace, pink and cream colored rose bouquets, sterling silver flatware, and my favorite Tuscan china from Italy. Voila! The terrace was transformed into an elegant outdoor dining area.

The meal, on the other hand, wasn't so simple. I agonized over the menu. Shellfish? Too many people are allergic. Chicken? Oh-so-boring (there's only so much honey and pineapple glaze you can use to dress up a skinny two-legged bird. I won't even think about the lemon juice and capers necessary to flavor an oven full of potentially dry-as-cardboard white meat). Beef, on the other hand, I thought, has always been a hit. After all, who doesn't enjoy the occasional decadent taste of a juicy steak? Beef is not as unhealthful as one might think; it's rich in vitamin B$_{12}$, zinc, and iron. Besides, a tenderloin of beef fits right in with today's high-protein dietary trend. I was sure my guests would be delighted if I served a succulent beef Wellington. It's a never-fail hit—cooked medium rare, wet, and juicy on the inside; toasted, buttery pie crust on the outside. It has always won me raves. I chose a few universally favored side dishes: buttery baby carrots, sautéed spinach, and steamed asparagus drizzled with balsamic vinegar and a spritz of olive oil—and everybody's favorite, roasted baby potatoes. I settled on individual chocolate soufflés for dessert. Hey, I warned you, this dinner was decadent and not for calorie counters.

We were smack dab in the middle of season two of my show, Growing Up Gotti, and my producers thought this party would make a great episode for the show. So, for the six hours I spent preparing my decorations, making tasty canapés, choosing the right red wines, wrapping up my Wellington, and tossing together the side dishes and dessert, I had a camera crew and sound technician following my every move—everything had to be perfect.

Even my youngest son, Frank, agreed to help out, donning a red waiter's jacket and agreeing to valet the cars. My best friend Rachel was also present to lend a hand. Good thing, because as luck would have it, my dinner guests began to arrive at 7:15. Seeing as they were nearly forty-five minutes early, I raced around the kitchen nearly tossing the fresh-from-the-oven mini crab puffs onto a silver platter and began serving the hors d'oeouvres myself. Of course, Carmelita, my somewhat lackadaisical housekeeper, was nowhere to be seen, though she knew I would be needing her help with the party. No doubt she was in her room, taking a late nap.

A word to the wise for those of you who insist upon arriving early—don't! Most times the hostess is simply way too polite to tell you it really does matter. As much as a host or hostess might want to say "Dinner at eight means 8:00, not 7:15, 7:30, or even 7:45," she'll purr, "Oh, it doesn't matter. I'm just finishing up a few last-minute tasks." Every second counts when preparing dinner for thirty all by yourself.

And please don't offer to help. More than likely, you'll be in the way. Besides, let's face it, you don't really want to roll up the sleeves of your new Oscar de la Renta cocktail dress and chance frizzing up your $250 Oribe blow-out, much less melting a layer of your perfectly applied MAC makeup.

I, on the other hand, looked completely frazzled! The golden curls that crowned my head less than an hour earlier were now wilted, frizzy locks; the makeup that had been artfully applied early that evening was beginning to run down the sides of my face, and even though the rest of the house was a cool and comfortable 71 degrees, the kitchen was a steam bath! Two ovens and two stovetops going at once raised the temperature at least 20 degrees. Did I mention the new Vera Wang evening pumps that now had a sauce spot at the tip of the left toe?

But I had no time to fret over my appearance. My new boss would be walking in the door any minute and I had to be ready. Rachel raced around the kitchen helping me. We've been pals for so long and had endured so many last-minute dinner parties and crises together, tonight seemed rather routine. I'd start a sentence; she'd finish it. I'd begin a task like straining the homemade cavatelli onto a platter while she began spooning sauce sparingly over the top.

Rachel placed the salmon toast points on a silver serving tray and passed them out to my early guests who were standing around the living room, bored beyond belief.

Hor d'oeuvres should actually be served to buy time for all the guests to arrive and the meal preparations to be finished. While everyone munched on the canapés and told bad jokes while trading salacious office gossip, I was trapped in the kitchen busily preparing to serve the first course—a tricolor salad with goat cheese and tangerine slices, garnished with chopped walnuts spritzed with a fruity, tart raspberry vinaigrette dressing. Of course my housekeeper was still missing in action. So I was left to fend for myself.

By 8:00 sharp, all the guests had arrived and taken their assigned seats. I'd gotten a bit creative earlier in the day (when it seemed like I had all the time in the world to pull off my party) and ran to Fortunoff's and picked up thirty miniature picture frames. I'd scoured my photo albums for appropriate pictures of each guest, setting up each delightful dinner favor in place of ordinary place cards. Judging by the oohs and ahs, the idea (one I'd borrowed from Martha Stewart) was a big hit.

Immediately following the salad, I served what I call my pièce de résistance, homemade, perfectly cooked pasta with my secret—and much complimented—Sunday gravy. Most guests wanted to lick their plates. Some even asked for seconds and, while there was plenty of pasta still in the pot on the stove, I pretended there was none left. A word to the wise: too many carbs can be overwhelming on the system and weigh your guests down. Trust me, there's nothing worse than sluggish dinner companions.

My first, and probably worst, crisis of the evening came about when I discovered there was not enough asparagus to evenly dish out to my guests. Apparently, the Italian grocer I often favor left out two of the three trays I'd ordered. When the groceries were delivered, there was so much going on I hadn't noticed the asparagus was missing, but needless to say, I noticed it now—right before I was serving up my entrée and, of course, I went into full panic mode.

In an anger-fueled whisper, I grilled my assistant. "Who left out the asparagus?" This started a game of pass the buck. The assistant blamed the driver, whose responsibility it was to pick up the order from the grocer; the driver blamed the housekeeper, whose job it was to put the groceries away; and the housekeeper, who speaks very little English, blamed me! "Maybe you forget. You put somewhere," was all she re-peated. I had made the terrible mistake of waking her from her usual dinnertime nap and boy was she in a bad mood!

Twenty minutes later and still no asparagus, I scoured the fridge and freezer for a replacement dish. I came up empty and there was only one solution. I had to ration what few asparagus I had into even smaller por-tions than I had planned—even if it meant only two spears per plate.

Luckily, my Wellington came out so perfectly and so delicious all eyes were on the star of the show. Carmelita had finally risen to the occasion and was helping serve my guests. She came into the kitchen, handed me a plate with an untouched portion of Wellington and said what sounded like, "Thees ees Hungarian."

I was too tired and too stressed to decipher what she was saying. My stomach was in such knots I couldn't eat. The rest of the dinner slipped by in a blur. While my guests dined heartily out on the terrace, I re-mained in the kitchen behind the double French doors, barely concealed by the billowing white moiré drapes, watching my guests through the miniblinds: Kathy, a stunning Russian gold digger, was busy turning up the charm on Jerry, my newly single, very wealthy childhood friend. Constance, the magazine's new beauty editor, a petite top-heavy blonde with bad teeth and way too much makeup, had an ear-to-ear smile while listening to David, the magazine's new managing editor. David bored the rest of the table with facts and figures surrounding a recent circula-tion report he'd read earlier in the day. And Laura, a demure Armani-clad brunette, recently hired as the magazine's head of ad sales, busied herself with a second slice of Wellington.

My new boss, the guest of honor, meanwhile was all smiles and savor-ing his third or fourth glass of Merlot. He looked like he was having a wonderful time, but where was his dinner plate? It was a picture-perfect scene, had it not been for the absence of my Wellington and that's when it hit me: what Carmelita had tried to tell me was "He is vegetarian!"

In one gulp I finished off an abandoned glass of Merlot someone had left sitting on the counter and made my way out to the terrace. I spent the next twenty minutes apologizing for my mistake. Had I taken the time, I would have known well in advance that my new boss was a vegetarian—in fact, he hadn't eaten meat in more than twenty years!

Embarrassingly, everyone else at the table already knew this—even my best friend Rachel. She remembered that it had come up when they were introduced at the launch party for my show two months ago the moment a scantily clad cocktail waitress appeared with a tray of carpaccio and he declined.

"Why didn't you tell me?" I demanded.

A visibly shaken Rachel responded, "Because you never asked . . . besides, I thought you knew. Everyone knows he doesn't eat meat." The dinner chatter got louder, I grew more nervous, tension began building up in my neck and moving down to my shoulders—a muscle spasm. Oh great!

I wanted to run in the house and hide. Perhaps no one would miss me, certainly not my new boss who, as a result of my screw-up, would be going home hungry.

Luckily, I usually spoil my guests when it comes to dessert and tonight was no exception as I served still warm miniature chocolate soufflés with lemon vanilla sauce and a dollop of fresh whipped cream. It was so delicious that one woman did her best Meg Ryan imitation from **When Harry Met Sally,** moaning a great fake orgasm after two spoonfuls, much to the other guests' delight. Another guest licked his small beige ramekin clean—literally—and another begged me for the recipe. Even my boss seemed overjoyed by the last dish I'd chosen. Talk about a real lifesaver!

INFORMAL AL FRESCO DINNER FOR FRIENDS

Antipasto

BREAD FILLED WITH FRESH CHEESE (page 33)

First Course

RIGATONI IN SUNDAY GRAVY (page 124 or 126)

Salad

TRICOLOR SALAD WITH GOAT CHEESE

AND RASPBERRY BALSAMIC VINAIGRETTE (page 18)

Main Course

BEEF WELLINGTON (page 119)

ITALIAN-STYLE HERBED BABY CARROTS (page 158)

ROASTED BABY POTATOES (page 154)

GRILLED ASPARAGUS VINAIGRETTE (page 156)

Dessert

CHOCOLATE SOUFFLÉ (page 193)

I can almost guarantee this tried-and-true dinner menu will leave your guests raving about your culinary expertise for months to come. In fact, I've found it so successful I made it when I entertained my new boss and several coworkers and friends (page 219).

GOTTI FAMILY REUNION

Antipasto

STUFFED SWEET PEPPERS (page 40)

First Course

RISOTTO WITH FRESH ASPARAGUS (page 89)

Or

ORRECCIETTE PASTA WITH BROCCOLI RABE

AND SAUSAGE (page 118)

Salad

STUFFED ARTICHOKES (page 44)

Main Course

ROAST LEG OF LAMB (page 212)

MAMA'S ITALIAN-STYLE POTATO-EGG SALAD (page 152)

ITALIAN-STYLE BUTTERED BABY CARROTS (page 159)

Dessert

ITALIAN CHEESECAKE (page 170)

If your family is anything like mine, food for any gathering must be delicious and plentiful. Here's a never-fail spread you can pull together in short order.

INFORMAL SUNDAY DINNER

Antipasto

SWEET MELON WITH PROSCIUTTO (page 39)

First Course

SUNDAY LASAGNA (page 214)

Salad

TOMATO, MOZZARELLA, AND

MIXED VEGETABLE SALAD (page 17)

Main Course

BAKED VEAL SHANK (page 111)

SAUTÉED VEGETABLES WITH GARLIC AND OIL (page 149)

Dessert

TIRAMISÚ (page 172)

I don't know which is more important for a typical informal Sunday dinner—great taste or quantity. As the person who does the cooking, I also want the meal to be simple to make, so I'm not chained to the stove while everyone else is watching TV or hanging around together outside.

GROWN-UP BIRTHDAY FEAST

Antipasto

BABY BRUSCHETTAS (page 48)

First Course

RIGATONI PASTA WITH TOMATO SAUCE (page 60)

Salad

SWEET MELON WITH PROSCIUTTO (page 39)

Main Course

STEAK WITH MARINARA SAUCE (page 116)

ITALIAN-STYLE SAUTÉED BROCCOLI RABE (page 161)

Dessert

ITALIAN LEMON ICE (page 181)

Not every birthday party has to be cake and ice cream. This exquisite sit-down dinner party is one of my favorite ways to celebrate the day for a spouse, a family member, or a friend. You're certain to impress with this menu.

SPRING BRIDAL SHOWER

Antipasto

**MOZZARELLA, TOMATO, AND BASIL SLICES
WITH BALSAMIC DRIZZLE** (page 49)

First Course

VEGETABLE RISOTTO (page 92)

Salad

**TRICOLOR SALAD WITH GOAT CHEESE
AND RASPBERRY BALSAMIC VINAIGRETTE** (page 18)

Main Course

CHICKEN ROLLATINI (page 82)

STUFFED SWEET PEPPERS (page 40)

ITALIAN-STYLE SAUTEÉD BROCCOLI RABE (page 161)

Dessert

CHOCOLATE SOUFFLÉ (page 193)

Last spring, I threw a shower for a newly engaged friend, inviting the bride-to-be and six close pals to lunch on the terrace. I decorated the large round table with a silver tablecloth and silver candelabras. As a centerpiece, I arranged fresh spring flowers—roses, tulips, and lilies in shades of yellow and white—and added silver chiffon around the brim of a breezy straw hat.

I repeated this spring hat motif by decorating smaller hats with roses around the brim and dangling them by lengths of chiffon down the back of each chair.

My menu was as fresh as spring, too.

WARM WINTER BRUNCH

Antipasto

STUFFED MUSHROOMS (page 41)

First Course

MAMA'S HOMEMADE CHICKEN SOUP (page 138)

Salad

SALAD WITH FONTINA CHEESE AND PEARS (page 14)

Main Course

VINEGARED PEPPERS AND PORK CHOPS (page 107)

SAUTÉED ESCAROLE (page 162)

ITALIAN-STYLE ROASTED ROSEMARY POTATOES (page 155)

Dessert

CHOCOLATE RICE PUDDING (page 191)

There's no better way to spend a wintry weekend than snuggled in front of a blazing fire with friends and family and feasting on a delicious leisurely brunch guaranteed to warm the heart and soul. After a blustery day on the ski slopes or clearing a path in front of the door, nothing warms the heart (and body!) better than a piping hot, hearty meal.

ROMANTIC DINNER FOR TWO

Antipasto

BABY BRUSCHETTAS (page 48)

First Course

PAPPARDELLE WITH TUNA SAUCE (page 99)

Salad

ARUGULA SALAD WITH ORANGES AND OLIVES (page 15)

Main Course

VEAL WITH HAM AND SAGE (page 115)

MARINATED EGGPLANT (page 146)

Dessert

PANNA COTTA (page 167)

Not every meal must be a gala spread for a crowd. Why not enjoy an intimate, romantic dinner for two with the one you love? This is one of my favorite feasts for all the senses.

NEW YEAR, NEW LIFE

It was fifteen minutes until midnight on New Year's Eve a few years ago. I was in the kitchen rinsing two and a half dozen champagne flutes and preparing a toast to say goodbye to another hectic, frantic year and say hello to one that I hoped would be filled with good health, prosperity, and goodwill.

I arranged the champagne flutes on a large antique silver tray, grabbed three bottles of chilled Cristal from the fridge and made a beeline for the formal living room where my children, my family, and those near and dear to me had gathered around the television to watch Dick Clark's New Year's Eve countdown, anticipating the blinding crystal ball set to drop over Times Square in a matter of minutes.

I was so caught up in the holiday cheer that I didn't hear the phone. My oldest son, Carmine, raced into the living room and handed me the phone. "Mom, it's Brooke Shields," he announced excitedly.

While Brooke and I are friends and often speak, I was quite surprised to hear from her on New Year's Eve—at a quarter to twelve, no less. My immediate reaction was that something was wrong, so imagine my surprise and joy when the beautiful and bubbly actress announced, "Victoria! I'm pregnant!"

Brooke was so excited I could feel her smiling right through the phone. It was no secret that Brooke and her hubby Chris Henchey had been through the wringer and back again attempting to conceive; trying every procedure and newly discovered medication had taken its toll on them. I was so happy for her.

Brooke and I chatted excitedly about pregnancy—bulging bellies and swollen ankles and the good stuff, such as being able to eat as much of our favorite foods as we wanted without guilt.

Brooke also told me she planned to take some time off from show business to concentrate on herself and her baby, and take care of all the preparations necessary for the little one's arrival.

I was working as an entertainment reporter at the *New York Post* at the time and it didn't take a rocket scientist to figure out Brooke Shields's pregnancy was one major front page story! So, I made sure that I got all the facts Brooke wanted me to include in the piece. She said that she called me because she wanted me to be the one to break the story. Me! Talk about a great way to start this reporter's New Year off right!

As much as I wanted to talk more to Brooke, I realized there were only thirty seconds before the ball would drop at Times Square. So I cut our conversation short and we wished each other a healthy and happy New Year and promised to touch base the following day as both she and I couldn't wait to tell the world, to scream it from the highest mountains, that Hollywood's own "Pretty Baby" was having a pretty baby of her own!

The meal I had prepared for my family that holiday evening was traditional in every respect, from the honey-glazed ham and my famous lasagna to the lentil soup, leg of lamb, and stuffed turkey with all the trimmings. And, while my dear friend Brooke Shields wasn't physically with us to enjoy the feast I'd specially prepared for my loved ones, she was definitely there in spirit. She had given me a great gift in that phone call. I felt honored to share in her news.

I felt as though it were my family's blessing as well to celebrate—and celebrate we did! That was the greatest New Year's gift I'd ever received. Family, friends, and good, hearty Italian food—could life get any better?

I hope that the recipes in this book, and the stories I've shared with you, have given you a similar sense of joy and contentment. There's nothing I like better than the thought of someone turning through these pages and deciding to make a filling Sunday gravy recipe for their children; or realizing that sexiness in the kitchen comes from the attitude of the cook, not the height of her heels; or that family is the most important thing in the world, and that a meal cooked with care and deep love is one of the best ways to show them. If you know anything about me from reading this book, you'll understand that I firmly believe all this! I hope you do, too. So get to your kitchen, get out your cutting boards and frying pans, and get cooking—and don't forget to enjoy yourself!

Mangia!

ACKNOWLEDGMENTS

This project, like every project before it, would not have been possible without the help of my "unsung heroes"—giving of their time, effort, knowledge, and patience.

There is no greater expert in the kitchen than my Mom, who has taught me the tricks of the trade, so to speak. The undeniable grace with which you, yourself, have navigated the kitchen for so many years, has served as the finest teaching exercise for me, instilling in me the importance of tradition, the need for patience, and the beauty of cooking as an art form, as no other tutor could.

To my Dad, John, for constantly pointing out the importance of heritage and tradition—and for teaching me that without persistence, there can only be trial and error, followed by defeat. You taught me that I could do anything, become anyone with a mix of hard work and perseverance.

To my children, Carmine, John, and Frank, without your patience—especially during the all-day-into-night crunching sessions to make deadline, time after time, I could not have written this book and all others before this. And without your appreciation, hunger, and anticipation, I wouldn't be able to prepare, create, and deliver delectable and mouthwatering dinners night after night. I love you all madly!

I would like to thank all the generous, kind, and caring people I came in contact with on my wonderful journey to the "motherland," Italy—a country like no other for architectural beauty, heartfelt compassion, and genuine tradition. I hope to visit again and again.

To my editor Doug Grad, for his valuable insight—he saw this project as a reality and pushed me toward completion without fanfare.

To my publisher, Judith Regan, without whom this project would not be possible—you make one heck of a mentor!

To all the willing (and not so willing) victims always there to sample my recipes and dishes, even before I got the hang of it, I made all the dishes with love.

To my assistant, Robert, I need not remind you of the crazy and late hours of cramming necessary to make this book possible. Our memories of Italy will never leave me—especially Positano and Capri—the Amalfi Coast—or should I say, "The Amalfi-close?"

INDEX

INDEX

INDEX

INDEX